M. 709.2 LON

KU-276-365

THIS BOOK IS THE PROPERTY
OF NAPIER UNIVERSITY.

WITHDRAWN

NAPIER UNIVERSITY LIBRARY
3 8042 00426 8270

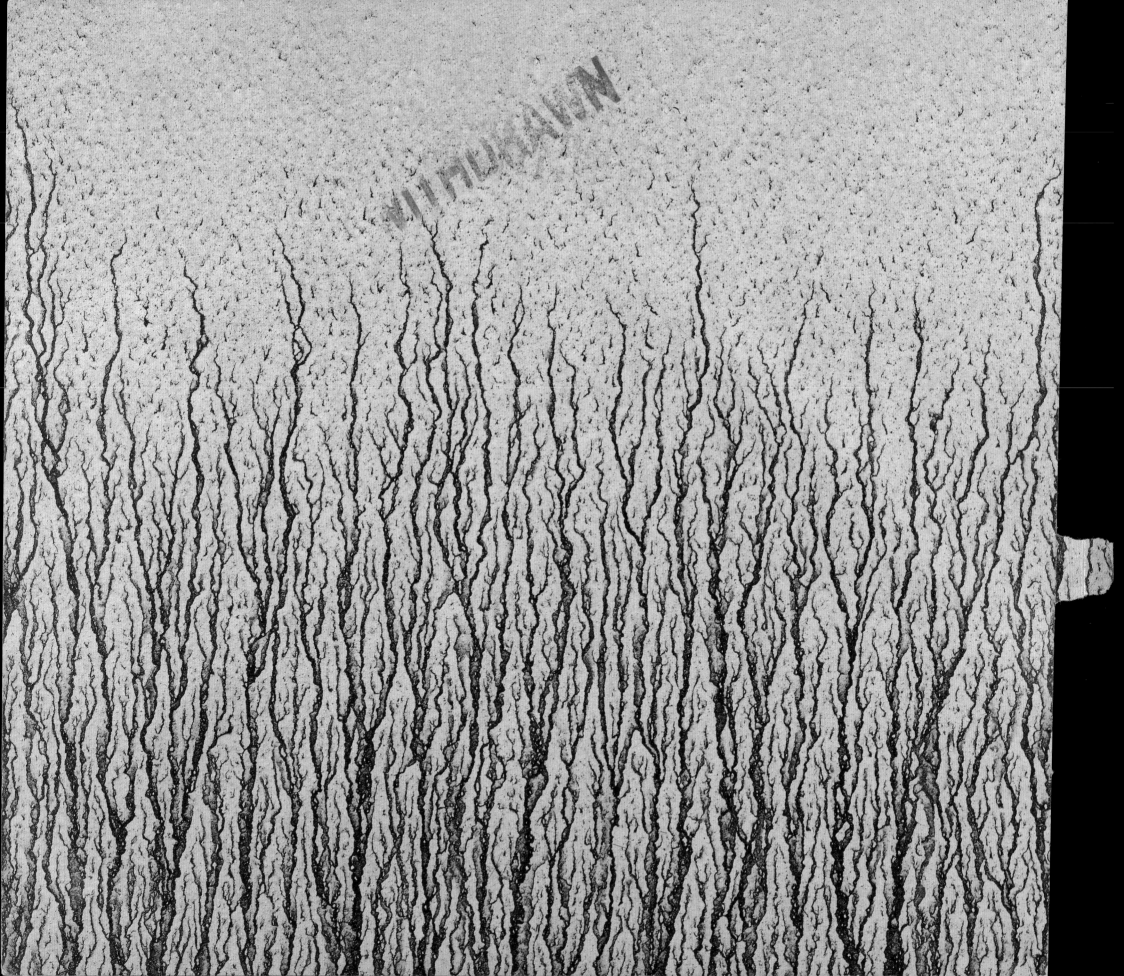
WITHDRAWN

WITHDRAWN

WITHDRAWN

RICHARD LONG

WALKING IN CIRCLES

THAMES AND HUDSON

WITHDRAWN

The titles of the first nine sections of this book and the sequence of the images have been chosen by the artist.

CONTENTS

WITHDRAWN

HOGGAR CIRCLE

WALKING IN CIRCLES

The conception and layout of this book are Richard Long's. The arrangement of the plates is not chronological and the text proceeds along its own route, so that images and words are like two walkers on the same road with different starting points and purposes, united only by the general nature of the way. Long is not the only person in history to create art out of walking, but he is one of the most remarkable. Like all moving objects, he is difficult to see clearly unless we move with him, and, like the gods, he is capable of sustaining many roles as well as that of artist, including traveller, explorer, pilgrim, shaman, magician, peripatetic poet, hill-walker and ordinary twentieth-century person from Bristol. In imagination we accompany him on his walks, but like most artists he remains virtually invisible. Occasionally we catch a glimpse of his shadow, rucksack or boots, but otherwise we identify with the traces of his passing, the spiral furrowed with the heel of his boot, the line on the map, the number of miles walked, the splash of the stone hitting water, the list of trees, the line of arrows marking the direction of the wind as it buffets his body. Whereas in Beuys's or Gilbert and George's work there is an aspect of their presence (in the art not the personal sense) which is important – they see nature through man – Long sees man through nature and reminds us of his presence by his absence.

This is a journey which takes the reader to the Sahara Desert and down the Rio Grande; from coast to coast of France and Spain to the edge of the Mississippi; from Dartmoor to the top of Honshu in Japan; to Bolivia, Nepal and the Pyrenees, among many other places near and far. It concerns time past and time present, the visible and the invisible. Passing through rain and sun, mud and snow, wind and water, dust and flies, from sea to mountain, down river and road, from forest to lake, up path and canyon, across moor and desert, it runs the whole gamut of sensation. Beneath an air of calm simplicity the viewer is bombarded with colours, sounds, sights and tactile experiences. But it is not all about far off lands and heroic distance. His own back garden, 'squelching', 'belching', 'laughter' and 'drying socks' are there on equal terms with Himalayan vastness. As Richard Long has said, 'My work is real not illusory or conceptual. It is about real stones, real time, real actions. I use the world as I find it.'

He once remarked that if he had not wanted to be an artist he could have become a cartographer. Of course in a sense he is just that, for artists are map-makers of consciousness and of the spiritual world as well as measurers and describers of the natural world, and their work demonstrates that consciousness is not divided one living thing from another, as the world is not so divided.

Some artists make the action of mapping and measuring a more explicit part of their work, Cézanne or Giacometti for example, but the activity of Pollock, de Kooning or Warhol is equally concerned with the same thing. Everyone's life is a map and everyone makes maps. A rosary is a map, a computer programme and Molloy's sixteen sucking stones are maps. A map is made so we can find our way from one place to another whether in nature or in the mind, not only once, but again and again. Maps record these visible and invisible paths which are created by various kinds of touching. Long has used the archetypal idea of the map to combine his natural pleasure in exploring the world with his understanding of its function in art.

It is said that the brain works in terms of ratio and proportion, in other words measurement. To trace its relationship to nature and reality the human body operates many simultaneous systems of measurement based on the senses. The human body has always been both a system of measurement and a map, both of without and within, a recorder of time and space. Long's use of it is perhaps part of one of the characteristic movements of this century, which C. G. Jung has described as an attempt to halt the war between the opposites of body and spirit, nature and culture, and to rediscover intuitively the basic facts of human nature, the positive aspects of our bodies.

Through his various ordinary actions, Long makes us conscious of the interpenetrating, interacting, moving world of nature, from trees to rivers, to the path of the

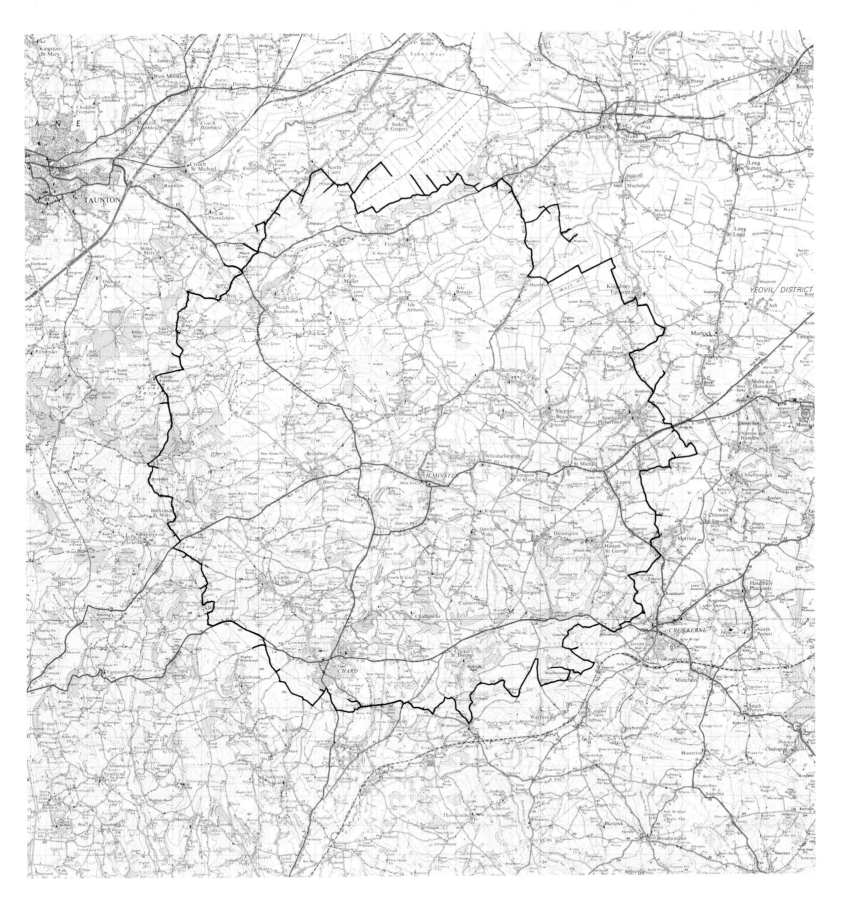

A WALK BY ALL ROADS AND LANES TOUCHING OR CROSSING AN IMAGINARY CIRCLE

SOMERSET ENGLAND 1977

THE HIGH PLAINS
A STRAIGHT HUNDRED MILE WALK ON THE CANADIAN PRAIRIE
1974

A MOVED LINE IN JAPAN

1983

PICKING UP   CARRYING   PLACING
ONE THING TO ANOTHER
ALONG A 35 MILE WALK
AT THE EDGE OF THE PACIFIC OCEAN

SHELL TO CRAB
CRAB TO FEATHER
FEATHER TO FISH
FISH TO BAMBOO
BAMBOO TO CARROT
CARROT TO PINE CONE
PINE CONE TO CHARCOAL
CHARCOAL TO JELLYFISH
JELLYFISH TO STICK
STICK TO SHELL
SHELL TO SHELL
SHELL TO SEAWEED
SEAWEED TO PEBBLE
PEBBLE TO DOG SKELETON
DOG SKELETON TO STICK
STICK TO MERMAID'S PURSE
MERMAID'S PURSE TO BAMBOO
BAMBOO TO CACTUS LEAF
CACTUS LEAF TO FLOWERS
FLOWERS TO LOG
LOG TO FEATHER
FEATHER TO PEBBLE
PEBBLE TO CROW
CROW TO CRAB
CRAB TO PEBBLE
PEBBLE TO THE END OF THE WALK

wind, the different cycles of existence of living things – in short, the entire visible and invisible flux of the structure of life. But the kind of movement which acts as a framework for all the others, and which we are most conscious of in his work, is that of walking, the archetypal symbol of human movement. This raises the whole notion of the body used as measure, which has been part of the classical tradition since antiquity when measure was recognized as fundamental. Then it was not seen as a comparison with some external standard, but as an essential inner kind of measure necessary for physical, social and mental well-being, a kind of insight into everything.

The return to basic principles, the re-examination of the language and ambition of art Long's work demonstrates, is part of a wider direction which gained new emphasis in the sixties and has sometimes been subsumed under the headings of Minimal Art and Conceptual Art. The work of many artists who fall into these categories (often expressed in terms of real space, ordinary objects, unimportant materials, words or photographs) also demonstrates a similar tendency towards simplicity, practicality and intuitiveness, and, above all, a sense of inner structure and balance which seems closely related to the original intuitive source of classical art in the human body.

One of Long's primary achievements has been to bring the body back into balance with nature in the most literal sense. Through the medium of his own body – fit but not super fit – he presents the moving, changing body of nature in all its tangibility and intangibility, visibility and invisibility, virtually unaltered and within the real space–time continuum we see as life. All this, as it were, passes through the narrow gauge of measurement of the human body, its sensibility and capability. It is very much like the camel and the eye of the needle. Long interacts with nature and nature with him and the results are eddies and vortices in its vast river. He uses nature 'with respect and freedom', making work 'for the land, not against it.' Unlike certain American 'land artists', he does not shift great quantities of earth or make permanent monumental works. He is the first to acknowledge that 'nature has more effect on me

FROM TREE TO TREE

PALM

CRAB APPLE 3 MILES

OAK 9 MILES

SCOTS PINE 15 MILES

HAWTHORN 22 MILES

WILLOW 29 MILES

HORSE CHESTNUT 33 MILES

LAUREL 45 MILES

HOLLY 53 MILES

ASH 58 MILES

YEW 60 MILES

COPPER BEECH 62 MILES

CEDAR OF LEBANON 70 MILES

SYCAMORE 71 MILES

REDWOOD 80 MILES

A WALK IN AVON

ENGLAND 1986

CHISOS CIRCLE
A TEN DAY WALK ALONG THE RIO GRANDE AND IN THE CHISOS MOUNTAINS
BIG BEND TEXAS 1990

THIRD CAMP EVENING

SKIMMING STONES ACROSS THE RIO GRANDE
ONE BOUNCE INTO MEXICO

A TEN DAY WALK IN BIG BEND

TEXAS 1990

than I on it.' In respecting and following the disciplines of nature he gains insight into the meanings of its processes.

Although firmly uninterested in theory, Long seems to have a remarkable grasp of the whole language of art, perhaps because he regards it quite rightly as a natural phenomenon. Looking back on the mid-sixties in *Words After the Fact* he wrote, 'the language and ambition of art were due for renewal. I felt art had barely recognized the natural landscapes which cover this planet, or had used the experiences those places could offer. Starting on my own doorstep and later spreading, part of my work since has been to try and engage this potential.' It is no surprise to find his starting point in the ground. Having seen a work by Noguchi, in the *54–64* exhibition at the Tate Gallery, which he felt was entirely about being on the floor, Long began creating sculptures on the ground, which not only articulated an indoor space but looked forward to his first outdoor work a few months later.

In art as in life the ground as the beginning and end of existence is literally and metaphorically of crucial importance. Whether in terms of canvas or clay or the fabric of the mind, the place you start from, the ground you stand on, where you make your first mark, there is always a starting point which affects the outcome of the undertaking. The ground gives balance and stability of focus, stops fragmentation of thought and has parallels in the need to be 'grounded' while meditating. Along the same lines it gets rid of inflated ideas and ego and puts the subject in a humble position in relation to the object of his intentions, allowing connection rather than confrontation. It offers a way of dealing directly with nature and all the forces which affect its rhythms and patterns. The artist of today may deny any specific purpose in his work, but intuitive preoccupations of this kind are some of the reasons the viewer continues to need art for its focussing, grounding, unifying and ultimately healing qualities, in the face of the tendency to fragmentation our particular time presents.

Aside from the energizing space and beauty of the world, the landscape is primarily a wide and open arena for Long's ideas. Invention is an important part of this, the fact that he is putting something into the world which was expressly not there before and is doing so without manipulation or influence. This is not to say his art is different in this respect from any other art, but rather that once again the role and structure of art is thrown into relief by the refining processes that go into making it. His sculptures are created in the likeness of nature, from its materials and using its scales of movement and time; they highlight the sense in which all works of art are a kind of flowering of human nature, and are as different and the same as every human being is different, and the same.

Long is interested in the emotional power of both ideas and images. He has also said that he has been 'conscious since the early days that each work should be very simple – like certain country and western singers, like Jimmie Rodgers, are simple in a very classic, artless way – but also simple in the sense of not taking very long to make.' The inference is that the idea itself has to be as simple and natural and similarly archetypal as the primal, geometric, 'natural' forms the artist uses as containers for his images.

Photograph, map or notebook echo the speed with which he grasps the idea. For the form born of the flash of intuition rather than the mechanical activity of memory, laboriousness won't do. Lightness of touch and quickness are of the essence to catch it on the wing, though once formulated the idea is tangible and forever. It becomes something which conceptually you can hold in your hand, or walk around if it gets too big, but which having been brought into the world, is there to explore *ad infinitum*. In just such ways Long may cause the River Avon to become a book or the Amazon Basin to become a tree, he may transfer a walk up Silbury Hill in Wiltshire to New York or create a room full of waterfalls by throwing buckets of muddy water at gallery walls. The transformation is substantiated by the reality of the means.

He has said, 'it's the touching and the meaning of the touching that matters', demonstrating that the sense of touch operates on every level of his work as it does in life. That was in 1971, when we were discussing the statement he had written for his

CHALK CIRCLE AND RIVER AVON MUD RING
THE SOLOMON R. GUGGENHEIM MUSEUM NEW YORK 1986

RED SLATE RING

THE SOLOMON R. GUGGENHEIM MUSEUM NEW YORK 1986

exhibition at the Whitechapel Art Gallery that year: 'From a mountain top in Africa/To a Tennessee riverbed, brushing through hoar frost/Magic signs, secret journeys/A portrait of the artist touching the earth.' At that time I interpreted it in rather a literal way, as the artist touching the earth with his hands or feet in order to make his mark on it, in order to make sculpture. I did not then fully grasp the extent of the reciprocal physical engagement with the natural world his work describes, whether through walking, water or mud works, photographs, words or rearranging natural materials. Yet it clearly demonstrates that touching is not only about hands or about walking, it is also about eyes, ears and mind. On top of a mountain in the Hoggar he clapped two flat stones together a thousand times. Touch, in whatever form, sets up eddies in the flux of life, which can continue to effect responses through time and space far beyond the original contact. Touch is also the primary means whereby Long effects the marriage between subject and object, viewer and nature. And as he has pointed out, not only does his work begin and end in nature, it is as natural for the artist to make art as it is for the viewer to receive it.

He has said, 'places give me the energy for ideas,' and elsewhere, 'I think I get my energy from being out on the road, having the world going past me.' Part of his work is created by walking and during the course of walks, and part brings the materials of nature to a more domestic or sheltered environment: museums, galleries, houses, the occasional hospital or garden. But both are made in the same spirit, just as the indoor and outdoor worlds are mutually dependent. He has told us the sculptures feed the senses and the walks the imagination. Either situation can involve a greater or lesser amount of physical activity, depending on the character of the space or the materials. Less energy might necessarily be expended on making something in a place it has taken a lot of energy to reach, comparatively more could be used to make an enormous stone sculpture in a museum. But equally he might just as well use a few sticks or pour some mud on the floor. It depends on the circumstances of the reality in which the artist finds himself. All Long's sculptures are in a sense stopping points on

FAST HAND CIRCLE

ANGLES GALLERY LOS ANGELES 1990

WHIRLWIND SPIRAL
THE SAHARA 1988

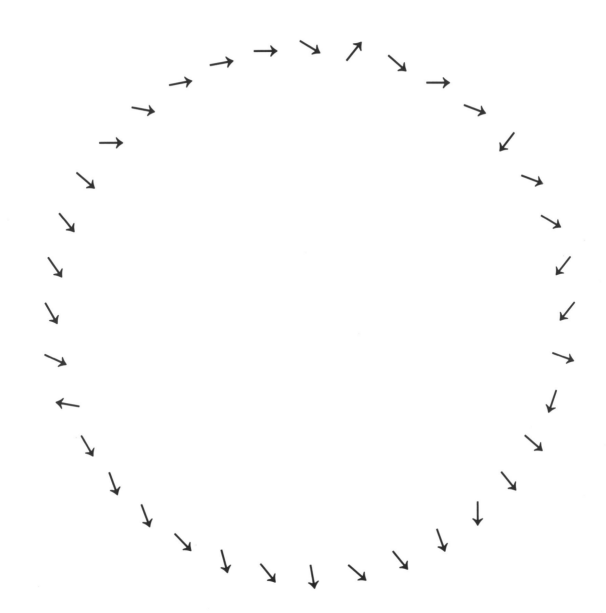

DARTMOOR WIND CIRCLE

A WALK EIGHT MILES WIDE

1988

a journey. They record a moment when everything feels in balance, and in such a place the activity of the artist and of nature seems to be doubly charged. Place and materials respond to the artist who approaches them in their own language. He seems to extract from them the explicitness of both time and eternity.

The idea of making something out of nothing and something which, in Long's words, is 'almost nothing' are both archetypal and heroic situations. When I first talked to him about his work he compared it to Beckett's character, Molloy, who kept his sixteen sucking stones in his pocket and just moved them around because it seemed the right thing to do. Long's sculptures in the landscape are made spontaneously in a few minutes with the residue of the energy remaining to him at that particular point. The work is seen merely as a brief visible moment at a resting place during an invisible journey, a knot in the handkerchief of memory, of the tie that binds, a punctuation mark or a sustained note, with all the fleetingness that implies. But it is also the visible residue or trace of the artist's activity, which becomes separated from him and continues to resonate as an idea even after, say, the circle of upright stones has been stood down and the artist and time have passed on.

There is something powerful, fascinating and mysterious about such residues, which are both essentially meagre and represent the measure of time and the condition of mortal life. In Hindu mythology, for example, Martanda, the father of mortal man and of death, was born from the residue of the sacrifice of rice offered by his mother Aditi. According to Stella Kramrisch, 'The remainder or residue is that which remains or subsists when everything else has come to a conclusion. If something is complete in itself, perfection, nothing is left over, there is an end of it. If there is a remainder there is no end to it. So the remainder is the germ and material cause for what subsists. It is the concrete reality of a thing.' The reference to the myth is of no relevance, but the creative parallel is curiously apt.

A remarkable, intuitive early example of this idea also involves two of Long's most important commitments – to the ground and to the path or track. One of his first

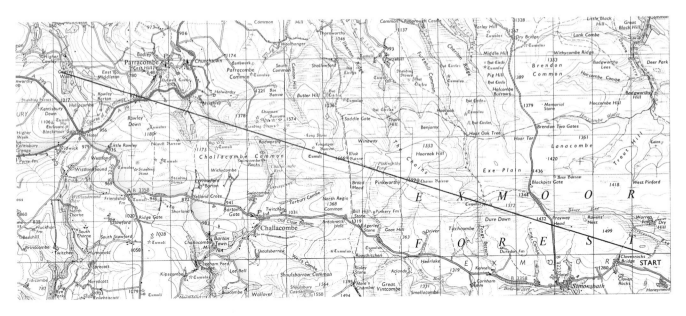

A TEN MILE WALK
ENGLAND 1968

works, done out of doors and dating from 1964, consists of a photograph of a snowball and its track. At the beginning of a long line of objects rolled, thrown or kicked this lumpy, rotating, roundish object was created basically of and by itself and its surroundings. It had a specific life cycle explicit in the traces of the journey which caused its existence and in the substance from which it was made. This idea of something made of almost nothing, containing both end and beginning simultaneously, as nearly as possible self-begotten, achieved with such simplicity and ease that it is both magic and mysterious, and in the making of which the artist appears to be simply the privileged transmitter, has been part of art since the beginning of time. Richard Long has found a way of using it to make art which reflects the human predicament in the late twentieth century with equal relevance.

If the sculpture is the residue of the walk, the path is the shadow of the body. When Long quotes from the Country and Western song 'Because you're mine I walk the line' in REFLECTIONS IN THE LITTLE PIGEON RIVER, GREAT SMOKEY MOUNTAINS, TENNESSEE, 1970, it is difficult not to imagine that one of the possible readings of 'the

A LINE MADE BY WALKING
ENGLAND 1967

A THOUSAND MILES
A THOUSAND HOURS

A CLOCKWISE WALK IN ENGLAND SUMMER 1974

tie that binds' is the archetypal image of the path. There is also a sense in which the artist not only walks the path or the line, but is the path itself. The path flows through him and from him. One of the defining characteristics of Richard Long's work is that it is simultaneously made up of quite separate analysable elements and at the same time utterly unified.

A path has a powerful energetic force – it marks a line of movement, a moving continuum between two places conditioned by the length of the path, the nature of the terrain and the relative speed of the walker. This is as true for Long's first path

through the room in the West of England College of Art in Bristol, as it is of the classic A LINE MADE BY WALKING of 1967, when he made a briefly visible line by walking to and fro across a field. Though the connection in the latter is more direct, in that the making of the work is part of the subject from the beginning.

If walking has become Richard Long's trademark, the path is perhaps the central image or archetype in his work. To walk a line is the easiest thing a human being can do to put his mark on a place. The idea of the path or way has meaning in all cultures from the most material to the most spiritual. It is both something real and something

TWO WALKS

The crossing place of the walks

start Ford Park

start

Walking time 2 hours 37 minutes

Walking time 2 hours 52 minutes

symbolic, something seen and unseen. To the Christian it is the Pilgrim's Way, the way, the truth and the life. To the Taoist it is the Great Way, the path into the light that seems dark, the path forward that seems to go back, the direct path that seems long. To the Zen Buddhist it is the Heavenly Way, *mushin*, the state in which the mind knows no obstructions, above the self, beyond thoughts of life and death, gain and loss, victory and defeat.

Long's images often suggest a seemingly infinite variety of linked meanings beyond what is actually offered by the artist. However, his works exist fundamentally as essences of themselves rather than references to anything else. They are quite simply facts – that is to say ideas which carry the process of their making within them. His paths can be coiled like a snake, meander like a river, or be direct as a compass bearing. They can go round and round like the hands of a clock, back and forth like a pendulum or speed before him down the bed of a stream. They can be as long as a thousand miles or as short as a few yards. They can follow a stone or follow the day. They can spread along a single track or be contained within a circle.

The important thing about a path is the movement and the nature of the track. It is a channel down which energy flows as the Avon fills and ebbs with the tide. It is the path of flash floods bringing debris down a canyon in Mexico and the same path explored by Richard Long. It is a path created by the footsteps of thousands of travellers and their animals over thousands of years between villages and over passes in the Himalayas, and it is the path that Richard Long takes along the same track.

A path can be one that takes you for a walk or one that you take. In A LINE MADE BY WALKING, Long created a new, virgin, straight track by repeated walking, temporarily flattening the field grass, so that from a particular angle it was possible to photograph the mark. A simple expression of the energy of man, it also seems like a simultaneous image of its own creation, of the walking body that created it and the pendulum swing that registers the time involved, and the sundial, speed-of-light element which fixes the image in the photograph that records it. Every path, like every work of art,

A THOUSAND STONES ADDED TO THE FOOTPATH CAIRN

ENGLAND 1974

has a mysterious sense of purpose about it, deriving from the traces of the energy of its making and the withdrawn presence of that energy.

As well as with a physical journey, artist and viewer are also involved with an inner journey. It may or may not be along the same path, but it nevertheless unites them in a perception of reality within or beyond the appearance of nature as it exists for its own purposes. This state of awareness, this sense of oneness between observer and observed, of the past and future unified in the present, comparable perhaps to the states of pure consciousness achieved by the yogic traditions (though there is nothing mystical or religious about Long's work) may apparently be triggered in the artist by the relaxing and focussing activity of walking itself. It is possible that the viewer responds to the residue of that energy, or that he reaches his enlightenment by identification or meditation induced by contemplation of the artist's idea. However we identify the source of understanding or the spark of illumination, what is important about it, in the historical context, is that in discovering art in a new likeness in the mid-1960s Long, whether intuitively or consciously or both, seems to have allowed for everything.

This book hopes to show some of the possibilities inherent in his particular vision of reality, which it is the artist's traditional role to demonstrate. In Richard Long's case this has been achieved through his own very personal choice of natural materials and images, while using ideas and language both as old as the hills and essentially appropriate to our own time and understanding. And just as, quite literally, he has broadened the horizons of art, so too he has broadened our perspective of its context.

For the purposes of this undertaking, the adventure begins and ends with mud, often thought to be the alpha and omega of existence. You cannot get more real than that nor more abstract. The endpapers of this book reproduce works on paper made from that traditionally primeval, fertile and life-giving, fluid combination of stones, water and energy. Between these curtains, these waterfalls, these pages of the River Avon, the artist has arranged a number of sequences of his work, divided into two main sections. The first contains examples of the constantly expanding inner core of historical works underlying each new achievement. This in turn is broken down into different preoccupations – a kind of naming of parts. The second, or outer ring, presents a comprehensive record of Long's activity since his last major book, published in 1986, on the occasion of his exhibition at the Guggenheim Museum in New York. But there is no sense here of the finality of the retrospective. This is very much a report on work in progress; the ripple has much wider to spread, the hub at the centre of this 'wheel of becoming' will still turn for a long time yet. It is hard to believe that the artist is only 45 years old.

In a moment of despair I once compared writing about Richard Long to the difficulty of describing a smooth round stone: wherever you begin, before you have got very far you find you are discussing something else. The development of his career is no exception to this fluid natural circularity. His work has grown steadily in daring, complexity and structure. However, since it does not follow a linear historical development, images are juxtaposed in this book to highlight ideas, similarities and distinctions across categories of time, space and substance. Because its structure is based on a small number of archetypal forms – the path or line, the cross, the circle, the spiral, the meander – and natural substances – water, stones, sticks, mud – and because the ideas tend to get developed many years after their first intuitive emergence into the mainstream of the work, the relationships between his sculptures are like a kind of dynamic four-dimensional round dance. Its patterns flow through, from the first paths and the stepping-stone sculpture done at the West of England College of Art, to the recent walks harnessing the passage of wind and rain, from the first holes dug in his parents' front garden, to his ploughing and stamping of spiral and circle in the Sahara Desert.

Bristol and its surrounding countryside is where Long acquired the language of his art (mud, water, stones) his first understanding of the rhythms of nature, the power of movement and time, and his love of walking, cycling and camping. Like all great

ROISIN DUBH
A Slow Air

A THOUSAND STONES MOVED ONE STEP FORWARD ALONG A SEVENTY FOUR MILE WALK IN COUNTY CLARE
IRELAND 1974

artists, he values the vision of childhood. He made his first plaster and water pieces about rivers in baking tins at the age of seven or eight. He has said, 'I don't think you can separate childhood from adulthood. I think you are the same person all through your life. So all the sensibilities that energize you as a child sort of flow through. And being an artist that means you can use them. So when newspapers derogatorily talk about my work as being sort of playing, like making mud pies or skimming stones across rivers or damming streams – all these childhood pursuits that people leave behind – I say "great!" I don't deny that I'm doing all the same stuff.'

Richard Long has not only managed to stave off the dead hand of custom which, as we age, falls upon our shoulders like heavy frost, as Wordsworth describes in his Ode on the Intimations of Immortality, his art helps defend him against it. His work seems steeped in intention to keep all channels of sensitivity open, to experience things as immediately and as keenly as possible, so that by simply remaining true to nature he will by natural means extend his explorations deeper and deeper into the nature of reality itself.

Just watching a river flow, Long has remarked, frees the mind, gives insight into the patterns of nature. Rivers and streams run though his work like arteries and veins, roaring through Himalayan gorges, their beds strewn with the debris of flash floods in Mexico, chattering over the stones on Dartmoor, poured like a sacrificial libation from a kettle onto the sands of the Sahara. Each has its own time-scale, its own life cycle. Long seems to sense an affinity between the Avon pursuing its course and his own journeys, and the glistening mud banks revealed at low tide are in a way the river's own sculpture. The traces of that gigantic, moving body of water passing to and fro to the sea like a huge water clock are perhaps not dissimilar to how he sees his own work.

There is a very real sense in which Bristol is the gate through which he enters the continuously renewed cycle of his activity. It is almost as if he is expelled by the tidal force of the river, and then pulled back again. Bristol is the place from whence

IRELAND 1967

A LINE THE LENGTH OF A STRAIGHT WALK FROM THE BOTTOM TO THE TOP OF SILBURY HILL (1970)
WHITECHAPEL ART GALLERY LONDON 1971

RIVER AVON MUD CIRCLES AND CHALK LINE (1984)

LILJEVALCHS KONSTHALL STOCKHOLM 1987

A SIX DAY WALK OVER ALL ROADS, LANES AND DOUBLE TRACKS INSIDE
A SIX MILE WIDE CIRCLE CENTRED ON THE GIANT OF CERNE ABBAS.

DORSET 1975

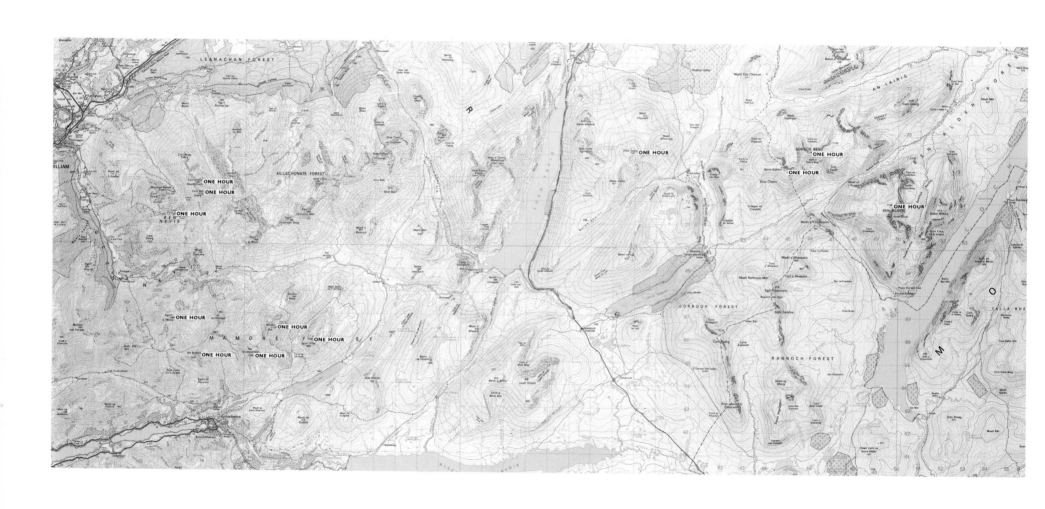

TWELVE HOURS   TWELVE SUMMITS

ONE HOUR AT EACH SUMMIT ALONG A 5 DAY WESTWARD WALK IN THE HIGHLANDS

BEN ALDER

AONACH BEAG

BEINN EIBHINN

CHNO DEARG

SGURR EILDE MÓR

BINNEIN MÓR

NA GRUAGAICHEAN

AM BODACH

SGURR A'MHÀIM

CARN MÓR DEARG

CARN DEARG MEADHONACH

BEN NEVIS

SCOTLAND 1983

FRAGMENTS OF A CONVERSATION I

For the 'daisies' [ENGLAND 1968], I remember having the idea to superimpose my own shape on a natural pattern of nature. I needed a piece of ground which had its own natural patterns, and daisies made a good black and white contrast. Then it was a question of looking around my locality and finding such a place. So in that particular example the idea came first. But I can think of plenty of works where I found the place first and then the idea followed, like SAHARA CIRCLE. But, by the time I made that, I was already carrying ideas in my head as part of my intellectual baggage – which is not so much to carry if it's only circles and lines! So now it's just a matter of finding the places, or being on a walk and being open-minded enough to let the walk and the place choose themselves.

Do you think that the work is there in a sense anyway, it's just a matter of finding it – like the simple tune you referred to?

Yes, just doing it. All those notes exist. You've just got to put them in the right order, like stones into a circle.

When did you get involved with Einstein's Theory of Relativity?

That was in college, in Bristol. We had to choose something to study for a term which would also be a programme for sculpture, and I chose the Theory of Relativity. The thing that came out of that was a path made of plaster. It was this idea of movement.

Was it to do with the idea that time and perception depend on the relative movement of the observer?

Yes, the viewer activated the work by walking on the path. That cropped up again in 'the square and the circle' [ENGLAND 1967]. In that work, the position of the viewer was very important. Instead of walking from one end to the other, there was one precise place for viewing the work, standing still, to do with alignment. So that place also was part of the sculpture. I suppose you can see parallels with how I sometimes take my photographs. Quite often there is an optimum place for looking at a sculpture, or the best place, the most interesting, the most visually dynamic.

It's like in one of the Carlos Castaneda books where everyone has to find their special place in the room. Somehow finding the right place is very important. I remember there was one chapter where he went to visit the home of a Mexican Indian, to be taught by him, and one of the first things he had to learn was to find his place in the room. You could also extend that by saying everything has its right place in the world. There are millions of stones in the world, and when I make a sculpture, all I do is just take a few of those stones and bring them together and put them in a circle and show you. So as well as finding the right place, you can also bring things together, hopefully in the right way, and say this is what the world is made of. This is a microcosm. This is one way to look at the world. This is my position.

And these things will still work even though they're out of water, so to speak?

Yes. All I have to do is bring them together into a circle. That's enough. Anything more and you're starting to change and manipulate the whole thing.

But I also have to say that I didn't have any of these ideas to begin with – thinking I'll use stones because I'm ordering the materials of the world. I use stones because I like stones or because they're easy to find, without being anything special, so common that you can find them anywhere. Again, it's the practical aspect. I don't have to have a special skill or talent for using them. I don't have to bring anything to them, I can just make a sculpture. I am not interested in representational art – that's art history. It's enough to use stones as stones, for what they are. I'm a realist.

ON MIDSUMMER'S DAY
A WESTWARD WALK
FROM STONEHENGE AT SUNRISE
TO GLASTONBURY BY SUNSET
FORTY FIVE MILES FOLLOWING THE DAY

1972

A FIVE DAY WALK

FIRST DAY TEN MILES

SECOND DAY TWENTY MILES

THIRD DAY THIRTY MILES

FOURTH DAY FORTY MILES

FIFTH DAY FIFTY MILES

TOTNES TO BRISTOL BY ROADS AND LANES

ENGLAND 1980

TEN MILE PLACES

A 206 MILE RANDOM WALK
IN SOMERSET DEVON DORSET WILTSHIRE AND AVON

A STRONG SMELL OF SILAGE
BENEATH A TREE DRIPPING MIST WATER
FLINT PEBBLES
A MOLE-HILL
AN IVY-COVERED WALL
MATING CHAFFINCHES
THE HARDY MONUMENT
CHALKY PLOUGHED GROUND
A TRAPPED SHEEP IN A BRAMBLE THICKET
A DRYING PUDDLE IN UNMARKED WET MUD
5 SHERBORNE YETMINSTER ½ MILESTONE
CATKINS UNDER A SCOTS PINE
A FIELD OF BLEATING SHEEP
BENEATH A ROOKERY OF SEVEN NESTS
FLAT DRY PATCHES OF MUD ON A SCRATCHED ROAD
A CRUSHED STICK A PIECE OF ORANGE STRING A POTHOLE
HORSESHOE PRINTS IN SANDY GROUND
SMOKE RISING STRAIGHT UP FROM A COTTAGE CHIMNEY
A SINGING SKYLARK TWO SHEEPDOGS
A FLAT DRY STRAIGHT EMPTY ROAD

ENGLAND 1986

STRAIGHT MILES AND MEANDERING MILES

A 294 MILE WALK FROM LAND'S END TO BRISTOL
WALKING NINE STRAIGHT MILES ALONG THE WAY

THE STRAIGHT MILES

CARNAQUIDDEN DOWNS CORNWALL

BROCKABARROW COMMON BODMIN MOOR

HURSTON RIDGE DARTMOOR

DUNKERY HILL EXMOOR

WILLS NECK QUANTOCK HILLS

THE FOSS WAY SOMERSET

QUEEN'S SEDGE MOOR SOMERSET

BERROW FLATS SOMERSET

DOLEBURY WARREN MENDIP HILLS

ENGLAND 1985

NAPIER UNIVERSITY L.I.S.

FRAGMENTS OF A CONVERSATION II

Are there works which you can pin down as being more spontaneous than others?

Oh yes, definitely. The LINE IN BOLIVIA (KICKED STONES) was a very spontaneous idea. At that particular place I started out by thinking that, as usual, I'd make a line by hand, but because it's kind of very flat rock and all these stones were interestingly scattered around anyway, it just seemed easier to kick them. At the moment of stooping to place the first stone, it just seemed easier, more practical.

The thing about those stones is they look as if they've been propelled. It's quite an explosive work.

Well, because it's a lava plain, when you kick stones they're going to roll. You couldn't kick stones in a field, on grass, or on earth. They wouldn't scatter in that way. I could only have made that work in that particular place. All works happen in a slightly different way. In CONNEMARA SCULPTURE, which is that maze, I'd gone to the museum in Dublin and had seen that particular image on an early rock carving, a sacred stone. I drew it in my notebook. Then, a week later, when I was in the west of Ireland and wanted to make a sculpture out of beach pebbles, I had that image in my notebook.

That's rather like carrying a stone in your pocket.

Right. But HALF-TIDE, the cross in Bertraghboy Bay, happened in another way. We'd camped on the foreshore when we came to that place in the evening. And the tide was out, and there was this beautiful bed of wet, soggy, bubbly seaweed on this stony beach, and I made a cross of stones on the seaweed. My idea for a sculpture was just to make a cross of stones on the seabed as the tide was out. When I woke up the next morning and unzipped the tent and looked out over the bay, the tide had come in, and instead of seeing my cross of stones, I actually saw the image of my work suspended on the surface of the water, because the stones were keeping the seaweed down. So that work was made miraculously a lot better by the tide coming in and covering it. That was a kind of amazing bonus. So it actually became a work about half-tide, because, of course, when the tide came up full, all the seaweed was completely under the water. You didn't see anything. You only saw the cross on the surface of the water at half-tide. Anyway, that was an example of a work that comes about by a sort of combination of what I do, plus some unforeseen natural phenomenon which actually transforms the work.

CONNEMARA SCULPTURE

IRELAND 1971

RAIN MILES

191 MILES TO 192 MILES

189 MILES TO 189$\frac{1}{2}$ MILES

187 MILES TO 187$\frac{1}{2}$ MILES

183 MILES TO 184$\frac{1}{2}$ MILES

178 MILES TO 179 MILES

174 MILES TO 175 MILES

170 MILES TO 171 MILES

159 MILES TO 162 MILES

153 MILES TO 158 MILES

113 MILES TO 114 MILES

109 MILES TO 111 MILES

89 MILES TO 90 MILES

61 MILES TO 64 MILES

THE MILES OF WALKING IN THE RAIN
ALONG A 203 MILE NORTHWARD WALK IN SIX DAYS
FROM CORK TO SLIGO

IRELAND 1989

A CIRCLE IN IRELAND

1975

A LINE OF 164 STONES
A WALK OF 164 MILES

A WALK ACROSS IRELAND, PLACING A NEARBY STONE ON THE ROAD AT EVERY MILE ALONG THE WAY.

CLARE	49 STONES
TIPPERARY	38 STONES
KILKENNY	27 STONES
LEIX	9 STONES
CARLOW	20 STONES
WICKLOW	21 STONES

1974

THROWING A STONE AROUND MACGILLYCUDDY'S REEKS

A 2$\frac{1}{2}$ DAY WALK   3628 THROWS

STARTING FROM WHERE I FOUND IT, I THREW A STONE, WALKED TO ITS LANDING PLACE AND FROM THERE THREW IT FORWARD AGAIN.
I CONTINUED THROWING THE STONE AND WALKING IN THIS WAY ON A CIRCULAR ROUTE, ENDING AT THE PLACE WHERE I FIRST PICKED UP THE STONE.

COUNTY KERRY IRELAND 1977

GRANITE LINE

SCATTERED ALONG A STRAIGHT 9 MILE LINE
223 STONES PLACED ON DARTMOOR

ENGLAND 1980

A LINE IN BOLIVIA

KICKED STONES

1981

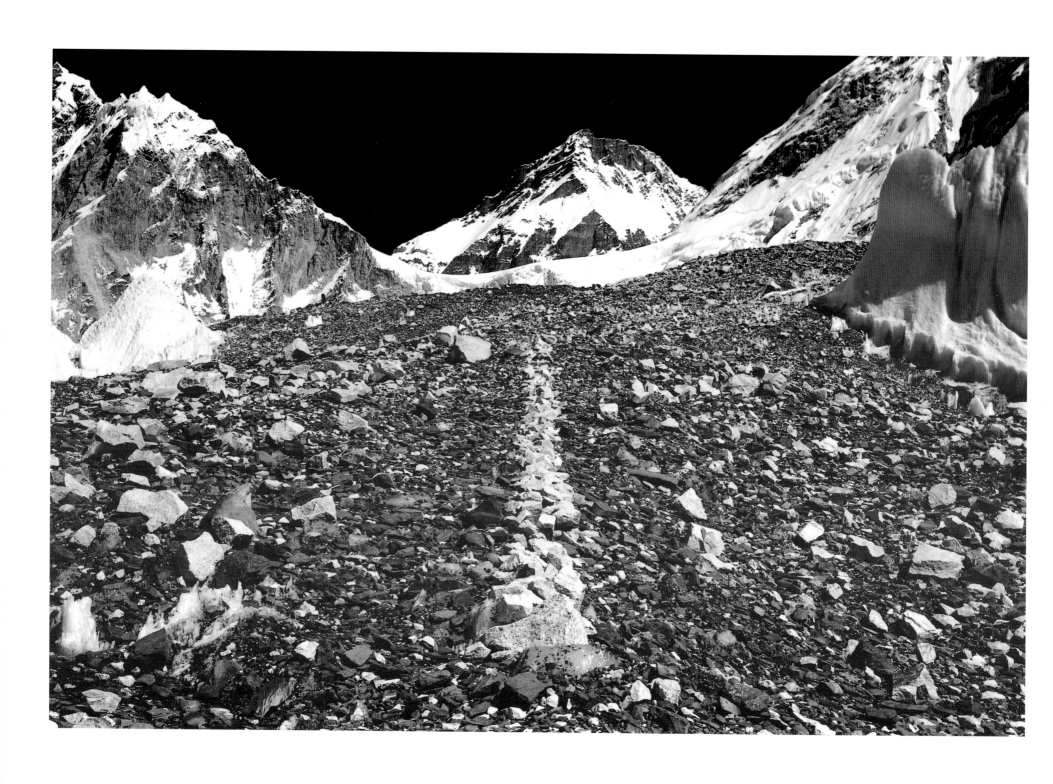

A LINE IN THE HIMALAYAS

1975

A LINE AND TRACKS IN BOLIVIA

1981

STONES IN JAPAN
1979

FRAGMENTS OF A CONVERSATION III

In WIND STONES *there is a feeling that your body is registering the wind – is that right?*

Well, the idea is that the wind is blowing every which way all over the place, but the stones only get turned along the walk, so it's about where I am, where the stones are, and what the wind is doing only at those moments when I stop on my walk.

TWO SAHARA STONES is about using stones to make music or sound. Somehow WIND STONES is the idea of using the wind as a raw material to make sculpture. It's tied in with the fact that in a wilderness place, like Lappland, one of the inescapable primal forces of a walk is often the wind. So the wind is blowing everyday, and I'm walking past millions of stones everyday, so in a way they're the two most natural things to be brought together.

The first time I had the idea to use the wind was the WIND LINE on Dartmoor. That was very much to do with the fact that not only does the wind blow from a prevailing part of the sky, but it also reflects the shape of the land. When you walk over a ridge you get the wind blowing at you from the opposite direction, because it's being sucked up over the ridge. Then sometimes, if you go behind a big boulder or a tor, the wind can be deflected in another direction because of it. So wind can blow in all different directions for different reasons to do with the shape of the land. I very much liked the idea that in a subtle way the wind line was also reflecting the shape of the land.

WIND STONES

LONG POINTED STONES

SCATTERED ALONG A 15 DAY WALK IN LAPPLAND
207 STONES TURNED TO POINT INTO THE WIND

1985

WIND LINE

A STRAIGHT TEN MILE NORTHWARD WALK ON DARTMOOR

1985

WIND LINE ACROSS ENGLAND

A 130 MILE WALK IN 3½ DAYS FROM THE IRISH SEA COAST TO THE NORTH SEA COAST
THE WIND DIRECTION AT EACH COAST AND AT EVERY TEN MILES ALONG THE WAY

1986

JUMP SHADOW GRASS ICE SCUFF SQUELCH SOFT BLUE BREATHE HOLLOW BANK RED POOL REEDS GURGLE SWISH REFLECTION SKYLINE BELCH TOR WIND DOWNHILL LOPING SUNLIGHT ROCK CRUNCHING TUSSOCKS HEATHER TWIST SQUELCH BUBBLING FLOODLINE SNIFF SLANT SQUINT SHEEP KICK CLITTER SLOPE GURGLING WATCHED SPLASH WARM MOTH HAZE LARK MOSS BROWNISH SKULL CAW STUB CAWING SLABS ALIGNED SPIDER SCRUNCH DROPPINGS SLITHER PANTING YELLOWISH

ONE HOUR

A SIXTY MINUTE CIRCLE WALK ON DARTMOOR 1984

CROSSING STONES

A STONE FROM ALDEBURGH BEACH ON THE EAST COAST CARRIED TO ABERYSTWYTH BEACH ON THE WEST COAST
A STONE FROM ABERYSTWYTH BEACH ON THE WEST COAST CARRIED TO ALDEBURGH BEACH ON THE EAST COAST

A 626 MILE WALK IN 20 DAYS

ENGLAND WALES ENGLAND

1987

STONES IN WALES
1979

STONES IN SWITZERLAND
1977

FRAGMENTS OF A CONVERSATION IV

It interests me very much that art functions as a kind of freedom. It's like an open point of view. You can invent any idea and that's enough – you can just do it.

I think the ideal state of mind to make a work in the landscape is to be very relaxed. I might be thinking of nothing, sort of absent-minded. I could have some music in my head. I don't think of future implications. I'm just involved in what I'm doing. It's like living in the moment. No past, no future. It doesn't always happen, but quite often the best works come from that state of mind, being absorbed and intuitive, sort of unselfconscious really.

On a walk in Nepal in 1983, the original idea was to follow the trail around Annapurna. To do that you have to cross a high pass – maybe it's not so high, about sixteen thousand feet – but the day before we were due to go over it the monsoon came early and blocked the pass with snow. Who knows what works I would have done if we'd followed our original plan. But the work I did after that was obviously determined by having to take a different route. I suppose everyone's life is, but my work in particular has to be adaptable, it's continuously changed, it's flexible. I think that's the important thing, that the parameters of my work are such that these changes and all those different phenomena are usable.

It's the same for the sculpture you make indoors isn't it? It can be moved from one place to another and be put together in different ways by someone who isn't yourself. There's a kind of trust there, I think.

But again it's also practical. If you're going to make a stone circle with maybe hundreds of stones, it's much easier, it makes much more sense, when you make it again if

A HUNDRED STICKS PLACED ON A BEAVER LODGE

A SIX DAY WALK IN THE ADIRONDACK MOUNTAINS,
THE FOOTPATH CROSSING BEAVER DAMS ALONG THE WAY.

NEW YORK 1985

WOOD CIRCLE

DELABOLE SLATE CIRCLE

ANTHONY d'OFFAY GALLERY LONDON 1981

PINE TREE BARK CIRCLE

FÜRSTENAU SWITZERLAND 1985

TEN DAYS WALKING AND SLEEPING ON NATURAL GROUND

BEINN A'CHAIT
BEINN DEARG
ELRIG'IC AN TOISICH
BEINN GHARBH
BEINN BHREAC
AN SLIGEARNACH
MEALL ODHAR
ALLT DAMH DUBH
LEATHAD AN TAOBHAIN
CARN AN FHÌDLEIR LORGAIDH
SRÒN NA BAN-RIGH
CAOCHAN DUBH
RIVER FESHIE
ALLT A'CHAORAINN
SCARSOCH BHEAG
CNAPAN GARBH
BYNACK BURN
BRÀIGH COIRE CAOCHAN NAN LAOGH
CARN GREANNACH
AN SCARSOCH
SRÒN NA MACRANAICH
ALLT A'CHAORAINN
LEACHDANN FÉITH SEASGACHAIN
CARN EALAR
MEALL TIONAIL
GLAS FÉITH BHEAG
SRÒN GHARBH
GLAS FÉITH MHÓR
MEALL TIONAIL NA BEINNE BRICE
LOCH MHAIRC
CARN A'CHIARAIDH
BEINN MHEADHONACH
FÉITH AN LOCHAIN
AONACH NA CLOICHE MÓIRE
BRÀIGH NAN CREAGAN BREAC
BRÀIGH CLAIS DAIMH
CARN A'CHLAMAIN
BRÀIGH SRÒN GHORM
SRÒN DUBH
MEALL DUBH-CHLAIS
TARF WATER
FÉITH UAINE MHÓR
MEALL TIONAIL
CONLACH MHÓR
BRÀIGH COIRE NA CONLAICH
AN SLIGEARNACH
TARF WATER
CNAPAN NAN LAOGH
AN SGARSOCH
BYNACK BURN
CNAPAN GARBH
SCARSOCH BHEAG
ALLT A'CHAORAINN
MEALL TIONAIL
RIVER FESHIE
LEATHAD AN TAOBHAIN
CARN EALAR
LEACHDANN FÉITH SEASGACHAIN
BRÀIGH SRÒN GHORM
AONACH NA CLOICHE MÓIRE
CARN A'CHLAMAIN
BRÀIGH NAN CREAGAN BREAC
FÉITH AN LOCHAIN
BEINN MHEADHONACH
CARN A'CHIARAIDH
ELRIG'IC AN TOISICH
BEINN DEARG
BEINN BHREAC
BEINN DEARG
BEINN A'CHAIT

A 134 MILE MEANDERING WALK

SCOTLAND 1986

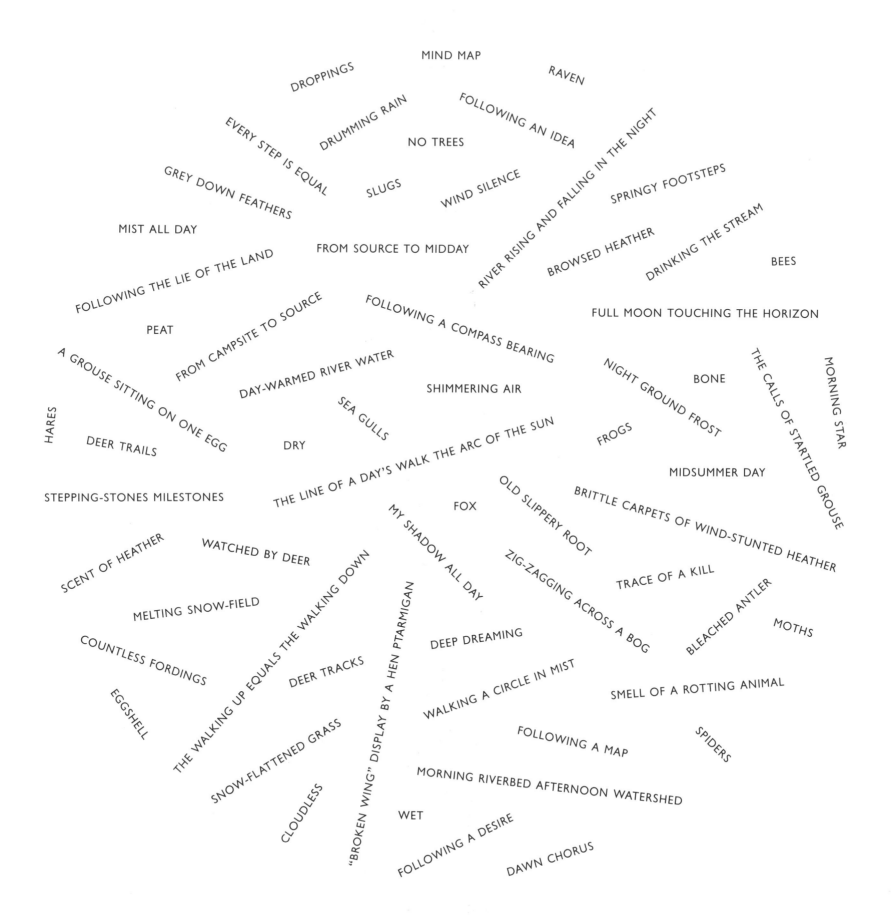

FRAGMENTS OF A CONVERSATION V

I think all my works, my actions, have no meaning outside what they are. So if you think it's significant, then it's significant. All I'm saying is I'm just putting that stone on the ground, though obviously I realize it's never as simple as that. But my works should be completely self-contained, they shouldn't need any explanations or references, they should be things or ideas in their own right. They should have a life of their own and take their chances. On the other hand, I wouldn't deny anything. The viewer can also bring things to the work, bring conclusions to it, which I could not foresee. But that's completely different from the artist making certain explanations and giving certain symbolic meanings to the work.

Did you ever do any kind of meditation, like transcendental meditation?

No. And I never studied Zen, which maybe is a wonderful way to study Zen. I take it as a compliment and a great fact of life about Zen and my work if people find similarities. I think there is a kind of underlying normal reality in the world. It's like nature. Nature belongs to no-one, but it's true in the same way for everyone.

I think one of the nice things I noticed about the *Magiciens de la Terre* exhibition in Paris was how much art all around the world is made by hand and on the floor with natural materials. I had an incredibly warm feeling about working like so many other artists from different cultures.

CAMP-SITE STONES . . . that's an example of a wilderness type of walk where I had a tent. There the tent also becomes an object of friendship, like an old friend. To make a sculpture where the tent is part of the sculpture is a nice acknowledgement of how important the tent is. Whereas PITCHING THE TENT – the idea behind that was every time you pitch your tent, when you choose the campsite, it's dependent on finding a level space, near water, out of the wind, sheltered. So all these factors make choosing a campsite quite interesting and pleasurable. It's like a very important part of the day, when you're tired and you come to the end of the walking. It's always good spending some time finding the right place for the tent. So I just used that idea. I thought, I'll make a work about the direction the tent is facing each night. In fact, out of that ten day walk that was the only work I did. So again it's like making a work of art out of some completely universal routine, which was also necessary and practical.

In many of your walks, the path of the walk is related to the path of rivers or streams, isn't it? In Mexico you walked up the canyon, crossing the river countless times.

Yes, in that case the river makes the only footpath through the mountains, and provides water to drink along the walk, and also water for water drawings, so there's a kind of circular logic. In CIRCLE OF CROSSING PLACES the idea was to make a circular walk on Dartmoor and just record all the rivers and streams and brooks that I crossed. It was the naming of the watery places. It was a sort of watery walk as a perfect circle. In DARTMOOR RIVERBEDS I used all the riverbeds as footpaths, within a large imaginary circle. An obscure piece of background information about the LINE IN YORKSHIRE is that it's in the area near Malham Tarn where the river goes underground. It just so happened that the river that disappears below Malham Tarn actually flows under that line. It's very typical limestone country, it's the same round here in Bristol. That's why the Gorge is full of caves.

HALF-TIDE

BERTRAGHBOY BAY

IRELAND 1971

DRY WALK

113 WALKING MILES
BETWEEN ONE SHOWER OF RAIN AND THE NEXT

AVON ENGLAND 1989

SHADOWS AND WATERMARKS

A MUD WALL BY A RESTING PLACE NEAR THE END OF A 21 DAY WALK IN NEPAL

1983

WALKING WITH THE RIVER'S ROAR

GREAT HIMALAYAN TIME   A LINE OF MOMENTS

MY FATHER   STARLIT SNOW

HUMAN TIME   FROZEN BOOTS

BREAKING TRAIL   CIRCLES OF A GREAT BIRD

COUNTLESS STONES   HAPPY ALERT BALANCED

PATHS OF SHARED FOOTMARKS   ATOMIC SILENCE

SLEEPING BY THE RIVER'S ROAR

WATERLINES

EACH DAY A WATERLINE
POURED FROM MY WATER BOTTLE
ALONG THE WALKING LINE

FROM THE ATLANTIC SHORE TO THE MEDITERRANEAN SHORE
A 560 MILE WALK IN 20½ DAYS ACROSS PORTUGAL AND SPAIN

1989

THE WET ROAD

THE TIMES OF WALKING ON THE RAIN-WETTED ROAD
ALONG A 19 DAY WALK OF 591 MILES
FROM THE NORTH COAST TO THE SOUTH COAST OF FRANCE

FIRST DAY 1½ HOURS

THIRD DAY 2¼ HOURS

TENTH DAY ¼ HOUR
ELEVENTH DAY ½ HOUR AND 4 HOURS
TWELFTH DAY ½ HOUR
THIRTEENTH DAY 1½ HOURS
FOURTEENTH DAY ½ HOUR AND ¼ HOUR AND 1 HOUR
FIFTEENTH DAY ¾ HOUR
SIXTEENTH DAY 6 HOURS

NINETEENTH DAY 1 HOUR

SPRING 1990

A CAIRN NEAR ERLETXE

A CAIRN NEAR MAEZTU

A CAIRN NEAR LARRAGA

A CAIRN NEAR SADABA

A CAIRN NEAR ALBELDA

A CAIRN NEAR TRAMACED   A CAIRN NEAR EL TARRÒS

A CAIRN NEAR LAS PEDROSAS

A CAIRN NEAR ELS CASSOTS
A CAIRN NEAR CANTALLOPS
A CAIRN NEAR GAVÁ

SPANISH STONES

A COAST TO COAST WALK OF 410 MILES IN FOURTEEN DAYS
FROM THE BAY OF BISCAY TO THE MEDITERRANEAN
MAKING CAIRNS OF WAYSIDE STONES ALONG THE WAY

EUZKADI TO CATALUNYA

1988

EUROPE ASIA STONES

A LINE OF STONES DROPPED INTO THE WATER FROM WEST TO EAST ACROSS THE BOSPHORUS
A LINE OF STONES DROPPED INTO THE WATER FROM EAST TO WEST ACROSS THE BOSPHORUS

ISTANBUL TURKEY 1989

MISSISSIPPI WATERLINE WALKING LINE
THREE DAYS WALKING ON THE ILLINOIS SHORE
1988

WATER WAY WALK

152 MILES SOUTHWARDS

WALES AND ENGLAND 1989

SPRING

AFON CIBI
RIVER USK
STREAM
STREAM
STREAM
STREAM

RIVER USK
STREAM

OLWAY BROOK
STREAM
STREAM
STREAM

MOUNTON BROOK
RIVER WYE
RIVER SEVERN

DITCH

STUP PILL

RIVER AVON
STREAM

LAND YEO
DRAIN
RIVER KENN
DITCH
DITCH

CONGRESBURY YEO

STREAM
TOWERHEAD BROOK
LOX YEO RIVER

RIVER AXE LOX YEO RIVER
OLD RIVER AXE

RIVER BRUE
DITCH
SOUTH DRAIN

KING'S SEDGEMOOR DRAIN

DITCH

DITCH
RIVER PARRETT
RIVER TONE

SEDGEMOOR OLD RHYNE
STREAM
STREAM
STREAM
STREAM

RIVER TALE
STREAM

STREAM
STREAM STREAM
RIVER CLYST
RIVER EXE
EXETER CANAL
STREAM

RIVER KENN
STREAM

DAWLISH WATER

RIVER TEIGN

STREAM
STREAM
STREAM
RIVER DART RIVER HEMS
WELL

FRAGMENTS OF A CONVERSATION VI

I just go from one work to the next. But the work builds up anyway. I am not naïve enough to think it's possible to make a work in the same state of divine grace, or whatever it was Rudi [Fuchs] said, as it was twenty years ago. More and more I keep intersecting my own past walks, all across England. There is no way I can go down to Dartmoor now and not be aware of what I've done there before. It's full of memories (one walk leads to another). I am aware of my own history now, and also other people's expectations, and how they receive what I'm doing now through knowing what I've done in the past.

It's like having notches on a stick.

I'm quite envious of people who don't have any notches on their sticks!

No responsibilities – you could just walk off into the distance.

Yes, pass through life without leaving a trace.

There seems to be a duality in your life about not leaving a trace and leaving a trace.

I suppose my work runs the whole gamut from being completely invisible and disappearing in seconds, like a water drawing, or dusty footprints, to a permanent work in a museum that maybe could last forever. The planet is full of unbelievably permanent things, like rock strata and tides, and yet full of impermanence like butterflies or the seaweed on the beach, which is in a new pattern every day for thousands of years. I would like to think my work reflects that beautiful complexity and reality.

It always amazes me that I can go down to Dartmoor for a walk, and even though it's a relatively small place and in the middle of a small crowded island, I can still spend a whole day walking without seeing anyone. But if I go to Nepal to make a walk, there is a social aspect, because I'm passing through villages, or staying in people's houses sometimes, or drinking tea in little teahouses. So on some walks I really do need villages and local people, for help or directions, or the odd great meal. Meeting some amazing character along the way can turn a whole walk.

When you make a line in one of those remote places, do you have a feeling about the energy of it, that it's not inert, it's doing something?

Yes. It's got to be the right thing. It's difficult to analyse. I wouldn't make any claims to be mystical. I think I get my energy from being out on the road, having the world going past me. That's the time when I'm conscious of the energy in the world and in me. I suppose that's the idea that some places are more potent than others. Each individual has his own preferences. But when I was on that mountaintop in the Hoggar, that seemed like an amazing focus of energy for me. That's not to say that mountaineers can't have the same kind of transcendental feeling when they're on top of a mountain. I'm sure they do. It's just I've made art about it by clapping stones together.

Was there something about the top of that mountain which made that sound extraordinarily appropriate?

It was just something I did. But I suppose it was the fact that the silence and the space were so big that it seemed appropriate to make a sound piece. In other words, I'm still using stones. It's like saying most people know that stones make sculpture, but you can also use stones to make music.

Did it sound almost insignificant?

Yes, like a cricket. Overall there was no real silence, but nevertheless it's like a small stone thrown into the ocean: it gets swallowed up immediately.

THIRTY SEVEN CAMPFIRES

TWO FRIENDS ON A THIRTEEN DAY WALK IN THE SIERRA TARAHUMARA
WALKING UP THE RIO URIQUE IN THE BARRANCA DEL COBRE FOR SIX DAYS ALONG THE WAY

MEXICO 1987

FINDING THE FIRST WATER INTO THE CANYON WITH THE LAST OF THE DAYLIGHT
A BOY BEATING A DRUM AS HE WALKS UP THE FOOTPATH YELLOW BUTTERFLIES
A GOOD STICK FOR RIVER CROSSINGS WHITE LIGHT OF A FULL MOON NIGHT
LYING BY THE CAMPFIRE A FROG HOPS ONTO MY LEG SPARKS AND SATELLITES
SITTING IN A WHIRLPOOL HOLLOW OF A WARM BOULDER WATCHING THE RIVER FLOW
CROUCHING ALONG TRAILS AMONGST THORN TREES A DRIFTWOOD BEND BELOW A HAWK'S PERCH
MUFFLED ECHOING SPLASHES OF STONES THROWN INTO THE RIVER BETWEEN CLIFFS SHOOTING STAR
A HIGH CAMP ON A STONE RIVERBED BY A TREE SPLITTING THE ROCK
TWO WATERMARKS BELOW TWO RAVENS BEFORE WALKING ON GETTING HIGHER COLDER WINDIER CLOUDIER
THE SMELL OF PINES THE PATTERN OF THE NEEDLES ON MY SLEEPING MAT
LYING IN COLD SUNSHINE DRINKING SOUP FOR LUNCH TALKING OF THIS AND THAT
DOWSING THE EMBERS AND LEAVING OUR RIVER STICKS ORION MOVING BETWEEN THE PINES
DUSTY FOOTPRINTS THROUGH SNOW SITTING WARM BENEATH THE SMOKE OF A CAVE FIRE

DRIFTWOOD BEND

MEXICO 1987

BARRANCA DEL COBRE WATERMARKS

MEXICO 1987

(detail)

TARAHUMARA CIRCLE

MEXICO 1987

FOOTPATH WATERLINE

MEXICO 1987

THROWING STONES INTO A CIRCLE
A SIX DAY WALK IN THE ATLAS MOUNTAINS
MOROCCO 1979

29

42

36

40

CORAL LINE

34

98 PIECES OF CORAL DROPPED INTO THE SEA IN A LINE
SAILING BETWEEN FRIGATE ISLAND AND PRASLIN ISLAND

36

SEYCHELLES

INDIAN OCEAN

41

1989

56

55

50   45

35

23

5

DEPTHS IN METRES

MADRID CIRCLE

PALACIO DE CRISTAL MADRID 1986

COAL LINE

BLACK AND WHITE RIVER AVON MUD LINE

CORNERHOUSE MANCHESTER 1987

CORNWALL CARRARA LINE

GALERIE KONRAD FISCHER DÜSSELDORF 1988

ELTERWATER STONE RING
ABBOT HALL ART GALLERY KENDAL 1985

GLARUS STANDING CIRCLE
GALERIE TSCHUDI GLARUS 1990

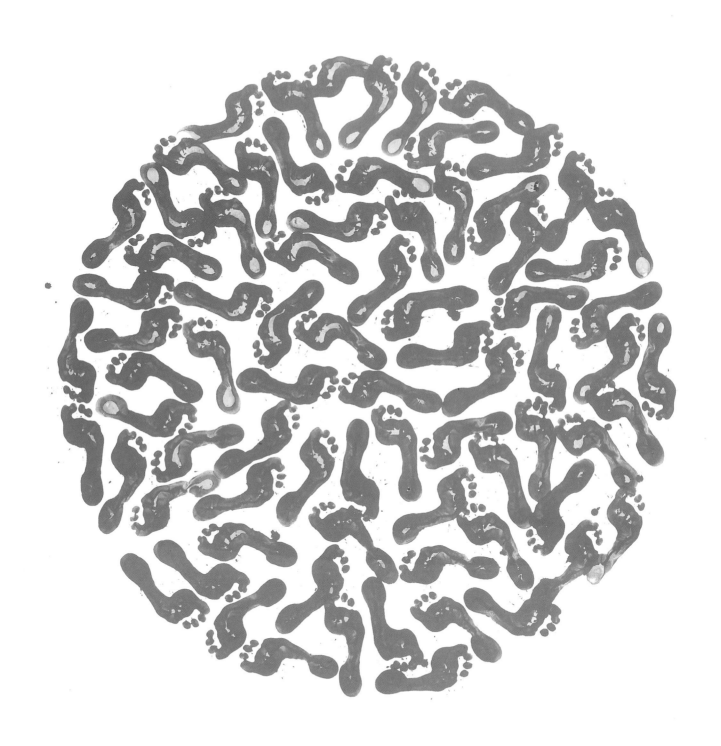

MUD FOOT CIRCLE

1985

UTAH CIRCLE

RED MUD LINE

LA JOLLA MUSEUM OF CONTEMPORARY ART 1989

Untitled SPERONE WESTWATER NEW YORK 1989

WATERLINE

SPERONE WESTWATER NEW YORK 1989

STONES IN THE PYRENEES

FRANCE 1986

A ROCK BY A RIVER

AN EIGHT DAY WALK IN THE PYRENEES

FRANCE 1986

FOOTPRINT CIRCLE

A 7 DAY WALK IN THE VALLE PELLICE

PIEMONTE ALPS ITALY 1989

WATERLINE

A 7 DAY WALK IN THE VALLE PELLICE

PIEMONTE ALPS ITALY 1989

DESERT FLOWERS

AN 8 DAY WALK ON THE HIGH DESERT
IN AND AROUND THE HEXIE MOUNTAINS

JOSHUA TREE SOUTHERN CALIFORNIA 1987

WALKING A CIRCLE IN DUST
NEAR KILAVUZLAR ON A 7 DAY WALK IN ANATOLIA
TURKEY 1989

ANATOLIA CIRCLE

A 7 DAY WALK IN TURKEY

1989

SPLASH SPLASH

SPLASH SPLASH

SPLASH SPLASH SPLASH

SPLASH

SPLASH SPLASH

SPLASH SPLASH

SPLASH

SPLASH

SPLASH SPLASH

SPLASH

SPLASH SPLASH SPLASH

SPLASH

SPLASH SPLASH SPLASH

SPLASH SPLASH SPLASH

SPLASH SPLASH

SPLASH

SPLASH

SPLASH

SPLASH
SPLASH

SPLASH

SPLASH

SPLASH
SPLASH
SPLASH

SPLASH

SPLASH

SPLASH
SPLASH
SPLASH

SPLASH
SPLASH

SPLASH
SPLASH

SPLASH

S T O N E
W A T E R
S O U N D

A 161 MILE WALK IN 5½ DAYS

FROM THE NORTH COAST TO THE SOUTH COAST OF WALES

A STONE THROWN INTO THE SEA AT EACH END OF THE WALK

AND INTO EACH RIVER CROSSED ALONG THE WAY

1990

RIO GRANDE CIRCLE
THIRD CAMP EVENING ON A TEN DAY WALK IN BIG BEND
TEXAS 1990

SILENCE CIRCLE
A RESTING PLACE ON A TEN DAY WALK
ALONG THE RIO GRANDE AND IN THE CHISOS MOUNTAINS
BIG BEND TEXAS 1990

SUN   DAMP DUST   COCK CROW   GUANO   COCO PLUM
CUMULUS   GRASS   SURF ROAR   ORANGE   SAND
BOUGAINVILLEA WARM WIND   COOING   COCONUT FIBRE   COCONUT
DOVES   PALM LEAVES   TRILLING   TREE TRUNK   RAINWATER
WHITE BIRDS   STONES   SCREECHING   ROCK PUDDLE   LICHEN
COCO DE MER   FERN   BIRD DROPPINGS   PINE BARK   CINNAMON BARK
LIZARD   BAMBOO LEAVES   CHIRPING   CINNAMON LEAF   ORANGE
CENTIPEDE   CORAL   HISSING WATER   CRAB   SALTWATER
BLUE FLOWERS   FOAM   BUZZING   PALM CATKINS   STONE
COCONUT HUSKS COBWEB   SWEEPING   TURTLE DROPPINGS SEED POD
MAGPIE   FLIES   FLAPPING   PAPAYA   MOSS
CHICKENS   ROOTS   RUSTLING   SAP
LILAC FLOWERS PINE NEEDLES   SEASHELL
YELLOW FLOWERS MOSQUITO BITE   BREATHING
BLUE FLY   GRANITE   ROCKING STONE
SURF   CACTUS SPIKES   BONJOUR
CRABS   ANT   GENERATOR
MOTH   LEAF LITTER   HISSING TURTLE
SPIDER   COCO DE MER BOWL   WHIRRING
SPRAY   SEAWATER
FOOTPRINTS
GOATS

EARLY MORNING SENSES TROPICAL ISLAND WALK

FRIGATE ISLAND INDIAN OCEAN 1989

RED SLATE CIRCLE

1988

RED SLATE CIRCLE

1988

SOMERSET WILLOW LINE

1980

Untitled JEAN BERNIER ATHENS 1989

RIVER AVON MUD HAND CIRCLES
ROSC DUBLIN 1984

KINBRACE
STONE FORT

TURF CUTTINGS
HALMADARIE BURN
ASLEEP ON BEN KLIBRECK   FOXGLOVES
CUCKOO SPIT

SRATH A' CHRÀISG
LARKS AND SILENCE
FULL STOMACH
LOCH SHIN

BITING FLIES
CATERPILLAR CAMP

BEN MORE ASSYNT
WHITE
YELLOW
BLUE
VIOLET
PINK

LOCH AILSH

FOX
RIVER BATH

COIRE A' CHAORUINN
COMPASS

RHIDORROCH FOREST
LOW RIVER WATER

GLEN DOUCHARY
A TEN HOUR SLEEP
ANTLER
THICK MIST
CRIMSON

SKIMMING STONES ON LOCH TUATH
SKIMMING STONES ON LOCH PRILLE
SKIMMING STONES ON LOCH NA STILL

FIRST RAIN

ORANGE MOON

FOX SMELL
SGURR MÓR

STAGS
LOCH FANNICH   TWO SOUPS
HALFWAY CAIRN   ORANGE LICHEN
LOCHROSQUE FOREST

FORDING THE RIVER MEIG

COIRE FIONNARACH

A HIGHLAND WALK

A 14 DAY SOUTHWARD WALK OF 244 MILES

SCOTLAND 1988

A PATCH OF SUNLIGHT

RANNOCH

SQUALLS

SQUELCHING
SLOSHING
SLIDING

INCHVUILT WOOD

WHITE WATER

CHISHOLM'S STONE

ABOVE THE CLOUDS
THROWING A STONE UP
TOLL CREAGACH
THROWING A STONE DOWN

GLEN AFFRIC
MIDGES

CEANNACROC FOREST
WADING

SEARCHING FOR THE PATH
PITCHING IN A DOWNPOUR

THINKING OF PERU

ALLT MHUIC
LOCH ARKAIG

CALEDONIAN CANAL

TWO BUZZARDS
THE SMELL OF PINE BARK

BEN NEVIS
THE HOOT OF AN OWL
THE FOOTPATH RAIN-WASHED OF FOOTPRINTS

MUDDY WATER LINE
GALLERIA TUCCI RUSSO TURIN 1989

FOOTPRINT LINE   GALLERIA TUCCI RUSSO TURIN 1989

WATERLINE

GALLERIA TUCCI RUSSO TURIN 1989

HOT ROCK
MELTING SNOW
WATERMARKS

A WALK OVER THE PRAGEL PASS
SWITZERLAND 1990

BOURGOGNE CIRCLE
GALERIE PIETRO SPARTA CHAGNY 1989

TWO CELTIC WALKS

FROM ST JUST TO TREAL FROM TRÉAL TO ST-JUST

CORNWALL   BRITTANY

1987

BRITTANY CIRCLE

DOMAINE DE KERGUEHENNEC 1986

TURF CIRCLES

JESUS COLLEGE CAMBRIDGE 1988

TURF CIRCLE

ARNOLFINI BRISTOL 1990

RIVER AVON MUD LINE

ARNOLFINI BRISTOL 1990

MUDDY WATER CIRCLE

THE HENRY MOORE SCULPTURE TRUST STUDIO HALIFAX 1989

COAL CIRCLE

THE HENRY MOORE SCULPTURE TRUST STUDIO HALIFAX 1989

HALIFAX SLATE CIRCLE
THE HENRY MOORE SCULPTURE TRUST STUDIO HALIFAX 1989

CORNWALL SLATE LINE

THE TATE GALLERY LONDON 1990

RED EARTH CIRCLE

MAGICIENS DE LA TERRE PARIS 1989

MUDDY FEET LINE

capcMUSÉE D'ART CONTEMPORAIN DE BORDEAUX 1990

GARONNE MUD BLACK CIRCLE

capcMUSÉE D'ART CONTEMPORAIN DE BORDEAUX 1990

MUD WALK

A 184 MILE WALK FROM THE MOUTH OF THE RIVER AVON
TO A SOURCE OF THE RIVER MERSEY
CASTING A HANDFUL OF RIVER AVON TIDAL MUD
INTO EACH OF THE RIVERS THAMES SEVERN TRENT AND MERSEY
ALONG THE WAY

ENGLAND 1987

WHITE FOOT CIRCLES

RED MUD CIRCLE
CHÂTEAU DE ROCHECHOUART 1990

RED MUD HAND CIRCLE   JEAN BERNIER ATHENS 1987

177

WHITE LIGHT WALK

RED LEAVES OF A JAPANESE MAPLE
ORANGE SUN AT 4 MILES
YELLOW PARSNIPS AT 23 MILES
GREEN RIVER SLIME AT 45 MILES
BLUE EYES OF A CHILD AT 56 MILES
INDIGO JUICE OF A BLACKBERRY AT 69 MILES
VIOLET WILD CYCLAMEN AT 72 MILES

AVON ENGLAND 1987

SEGOVIA SLATE CIRCLES
PALACIO DE CRISTAL MADRID 1986

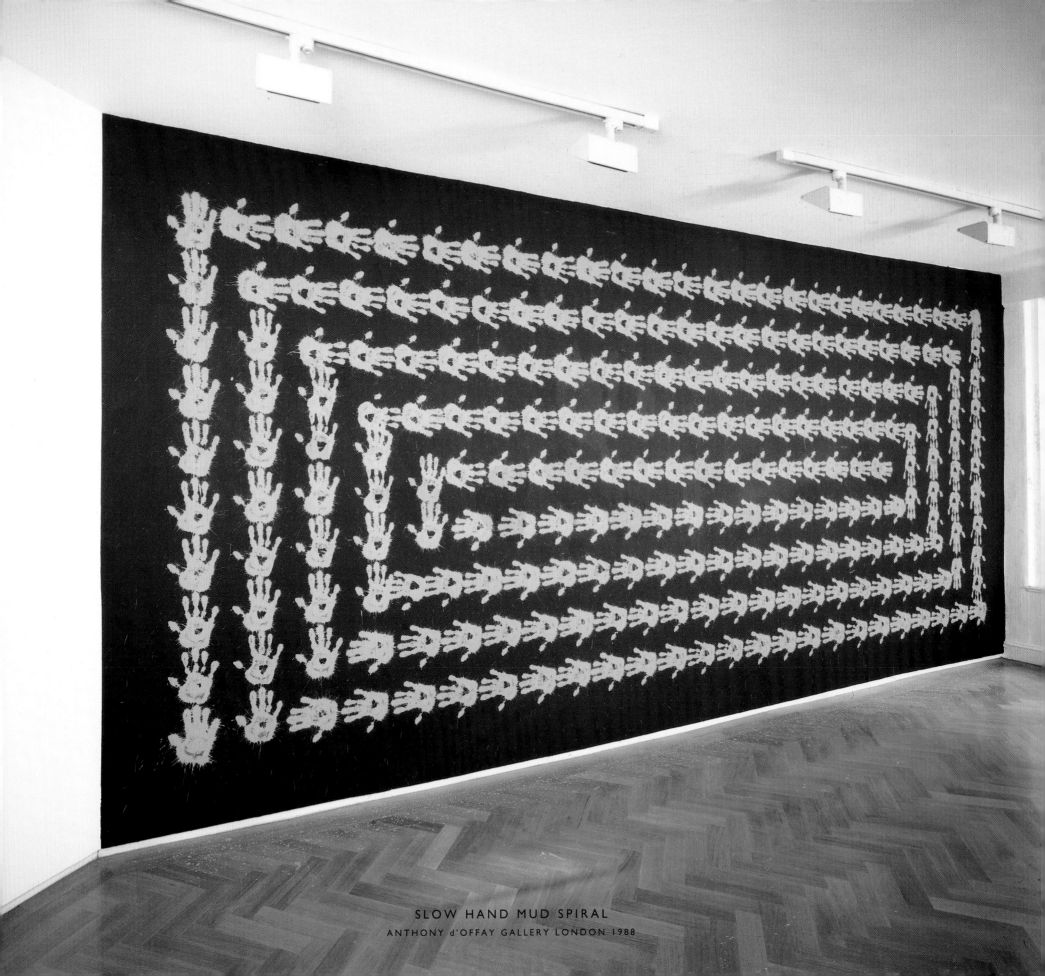

SLOW HAND MUD SPIRAL
ANTHONY d'OFFAY GALLERY LONDON 1988

A DARTMOOR WALK

EIGHT DAYS
ENGLAND 1987

DEEP BREATHING TO GRIMSPOUND TO BENNETT'S CROSS TO MIDGES TO A NEW-BORN CALF
TO GREAT KNEESET TO A LARK ON A BOULDER TO COTTON GRASS TO THINKING TO A FOX SMELL
TO GREAT LINKS TOR TO RIVER FROTH TO DOZING TO SWEATING TO YES TOR
TO A STONE CIRCLE TO SHELLEY POOL TO WINDLESS DAWN TO ENERGY TO BLUE FLOWERS
TO A BUZZARD TO HANGINGSTONE HILL TO SOUTH TAVY HEAD TO WEST DART HEAD
TO BEARDOWN MAN TO MUSHROOMS TO CUCKOO TO A STONE ROW TO CUCKOO ROCK
TO A WHITE BONE TO GREAT GNATS' HEAD TO ERME HEAD TO A MOUND TO DRYING SOCKS
TO YEALM HEAD TO DEW-SOAKED TO A CLAPPER BRIDGE TO FLIES TO BARROWS
TO A DEAD SHEEP TO THE WHOOSH OF A PEREGRINE TO SITTING TO TINNER'S STONES TO A RAINSTORM
TO A HERON TO SCATTERED BONES TO MOONLIGHT TO DRYING THE TENT TO TAW HEAD
TO EAST DART HEAD TO TEIGN HEAD TO A CLOUD BURST TO THUNDER TO LONG STONE
TO PONIES DRINKING TO HAILSTONES TO LIGHTNING TO GOOD MEMORIES TO A ROTTING SHEEP
TO VIOLET FLOWERS TO AN OAK TREE TO AVON HEAD TO A SMALL STONE TO MISSISSIPPI RIVER BLUES
TO ROLLING THUNDER TO A FLY IN THE EYE TO NAKER'S HILL IN A SQUALL TO PLYM HEAD
TO SHEEP'S TOR TO BLUEBELLS TO BELLOWING CATTLE TO WHITE BLOSSOM TO A FARMYARD
TO A BROWN BULL TO DARTMEET TO COFFIN STONE TO CAWING TO HAMELDOWN CAIRN
TO A STRAND OF WOOL TO THE SMELL OF NEW BRACKEN TO MOTIONLESS TO PINE NEEDLES
TO STEPPING-STONES TO HUCCABY RING TO LAUGHTER TOR TO GOOD FEELINGS

A CIRCLE IN SCOTLAND

1986

RIVERS   LAKES   SWAMPS

LOW SKIES   LONG SLEEPS   WET FEET

FULL MOON   A CANDLE   THROWING WATER

NO DIRECTION KNOWN   NO PEOPLE   NO WOMAN NO CRY

SLIPPERY ROCKS   BLUEBERRY-STAINED SNOW   OHTSEJOHKA

A 7 DAY WILDERNESS WALK IN LAPPLAND

1983

SLEEPING MARK

THROWING WATER

EAST OKEMENT RIVER

BLACK-A-VEN BROOK   RIVER TAW

RED-A-VEN BROOK   RAYBARROW POOL

WEST OKEMENT RIVER   LEAT

AMICOMBE BROOK   WALLA BROOK

BLACK RIDGE BROOK   NORTH TEIGN RIVER

CUT COMBE WATER   STREAM

EAST DART RIVER   STREAM

NORTH TEIGN RIVER   NORTH TEIGN RIVER

                LEAT   MANGA BROOK

                        STREAM

CIRCLE OF CROSSING PLACES

A DAY'S WALK ON DARTMOOR

1981

WALKING A CIRCLE IN MIST

SCOTLAND 1986

CAMP-SITE STONES
SIERRA NEVADA
SPAIN 1985

PITCHING THE TENT

FIRST NIGHT SECOND NIGHT THIRD NIGHT FOURTH NIGHT FIFTH NIGHT SIXTH NIGHT SEVENTH NIGHT EIGHTH NIGHT NINTH NIGHT TENTH NIGHT

TEN NIGHTS — TEN CAMPING PLACES

THE DIRECTION OF MY TENT AND MY SLEEPING PLACE EACH NIGHT
ALONG A TEN DAY WINTER WALK IN THE DAUPHINÉ ALPS

FRANCE 1987

SLEEPING PLACE MARK

A NIGHT OF GRUNTING DEER   A FROSTY MORNING

THE SEVENTEENTH NIGHT OF A 21 DAY WALK FROM THE NORTH COAST TO THE SOUTH COAST OF SPAIN

RIBADESELLA TO MÁLAGA 1990

RESTING PLACE STONES

A SIX DAY WALK IN THE HOGGAR

THE SAHARA 1988

193

STONE LAKE SCHIEFER-SEE

SCHLOSS CROTTORF 1988

COAL LINE MAGASIN GRENOBLE 1987

STONE FIELD ALLOTMENT ONE LIVERPOOL 1987

PIANOS

GOODNIGHT

SMOKE WALNUT PLUG

TROOPS OUT

WINDS GUSTING VISIBILITY GOOD EXCEPT IN THE SHOWERS

CÚIL MHAOIL COLLOONEY

A GIRL WITH FOUR COWS

PEACE SHRINE

KIELTY'S ROCK BAR

SLIGEACH SLIGO 15½

RAINBOW

HANGING OUT THE WASHING

HEDGING AND DITCHING

TRADITIONAL WITH JOE McCOLL

THE GURTEEN FORGE

RAINBOW

VOTE YES

TWO BICYCLES PARKED IN A HEDGE

KICKING A STONE ALONG SIX TIMES

ITS NICE TODAY

RAINBOW

CLOONFAD CROSSROADS

JESUS MERCY MARY HELP

THOMAS O'CARA R.I.P.

RAINBOW

SEAN QUINN CONCRETE BLOCKS

RAINBOW

THERE'S TULLY'S ITS ITS MORE THAN A HALF MILE LESS THAN A MILE

HALLO A BAD EVENING

LOTTERY

DIVILLY'S BAR

MANNIONS EVERY SAT NIGHT

ROLLED BARLEY JOYCE AND SONS

BIRD SANCTUARY

SHEEP MART EVERY SAT 11 A.M. SHARP

CONNEELYS LOUNGE

MOBILE LIBRARY

KICKING A STONE ALONG FIVE TIMES

GLEANN NA MADADH GLENAMADDY

GRAND MORNING

NO DUMPING

A CIRCLE OF BEECHES AND OAKS

NET NITRATE

A CAMP NEAR GORTEEN

MY MOTHER NEVER LET ANYONE PASS HER DOOR WITHOUT FEEDING THEM

ST. KERRIL'S WELL

ATTHMON PEAT CO-OP

RAFTERY'S

GROCERY PROVISIONS MEALS FLOUR

THE THREE LEAF SHAMROCKS

A DARK MORNING

A CAMP IN THE SLIEVE AUGHTY MOUNTAINS

KICKING A STONE ALONG THREE TIMES

AN FHIACAIL FEAKLE

IASCAIREACHT FISHING

RING FORT

UNEVEN SURFACE

RIVER VALLEY LOUNGE BALLADS SNACKS

FÁILTE GO CO. AN CHLÁIR WELCOME TO COUNTY CLARE

CHILDREN GOING TO SCHOOL

LIMERICK

TEMPORARY DWELLINGS PROHIBITED

WHO'S HE?

SANCTUARY NO SHOOTING

THE STROLLER

BALLYNEETY

LAND POISONED

THE GREAT STONE CIRCLE AN MÓRCHIORCAL CLOCH

CABBAGE PLANTS FOR SALE

BRÚ NA N DEISE A TIDY TOWN

KICKING A STONE ALONG TWICE

SOFT MARGIN

CAUTION COWS CROSSING

LIVE MUSIC DANCING

A CAMP IN THE BALLYHOURA MOUNTAINS

BLACKBERRY-STAINED FINGERS

KICKING A STONE ALONG ONCE

SIXMILEWATER

CARRAIG NA BHFEAR

START

FINISH

CORK METAL CO

SNORING

KICKING STONES

A 203 MILE NORTHWARD WALK IN SIX DAYS

CORK TO SLIGO

IRELAND 1989

WHITE ROCK LINE

capcMUSÉE D'ART CONTEMPORAIN DE BORDEAUX 1990

GARONNE MUD CIRCLES

capcMUSÉE D'ART CONTEMPORAIN DE BORDEAUX 1990

WHITE MUD CIRCLE
CHÂTEAU DE ROCHECHOUART 1990

MUDDY FEET CIRCLE

CHÂTEAU DE ROCHECHOUART 1990

ROCHECHOUART CIRCLE

CHÂTEAU DE ROCHECHOUART 1990

ROCHECHOUART LINE
CHÂTEAU DE ROCHECHOUART 1990

ALPINE CIRCLE

CHÂTEAU DE ROCHECHOUART 1990

ON THE ROAD

SOMETHING SEEN AND PASSED EACH DAY
ALONG A 19 DAY WALK OF 591 MILES
FROM THE NORTH COAST TO THE SOUTH COAST OF FRANCE

A PIECE OF FLINT IN DIEPPE

A PIECE OF FLINT IN Sᵀ-PIERRE-DES-FLEURS

A SCREWDRIVER NEAR LA BROSSE

A WHITE FEATHER IN LA FRAMBOISIÈRE

A BICYCLE CHAIN NEAR YÈVRES

A SHOE IN BEAUGENCY

A SILVER COIN IN Sᵀ-JULIEN-SUR-CHER

A BONE NEAR ISSOUDUN

A DEAD SNAKE NEAR NOHANT-VIC

A CATERPILLAR NEAR BEAUREGARD

A BOUQUET OF FLOWERS IN CROZE

A POTATO NEAR NEUVIC

A COMIC IN Sᵀ-MARTIN-VALMEROUX

A SNAIL NEAR MONTSALVY

A TAPE CASSETTE IN ENTRAYGUES-SUR-TRUYÈRE

A DANDELION NEAR DOUZOUMAYROUX

A PIECE OF LIMESTONE IN L'HOSPITALET-DU-LARZAC

A NOTEBOOK IN LE PAS-DE-L'ESCALETTE

A BUTTERFLY NEAR BESSAN

1990

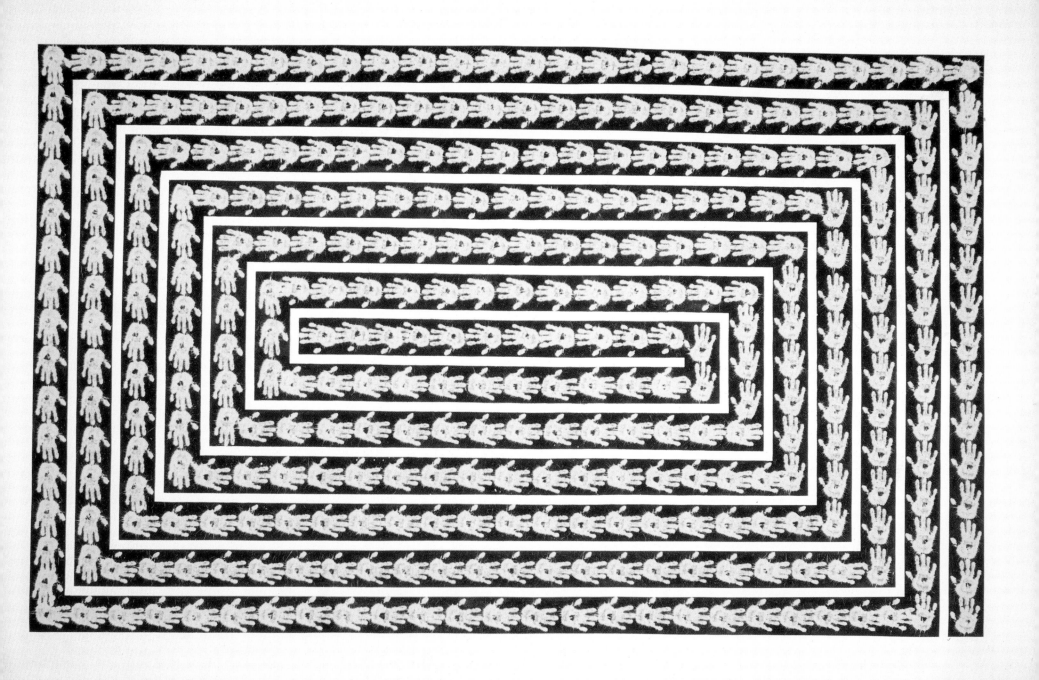

WHITE HAND SPIRAL
CHÂTEAU DE ROCHECHOUART 1990

WATER CIRCLES

WHITE WATER LINE · THE TATE GALLERY LONDON 1990

NORFOLK FLINT CIRCLE AND WHITE WATER LINE

THE TATE GALLERY LONDON 1990

SLOW HAND CIRCLES

ANGLES GALLERY LOS ANGELES 1990

OCEAN STONE CIRCLE

ANGLES GALLERY LOS ANGELES 1990

TWO SAHARA STONES

SITTING ON A MOUNTAINTOP
IN THE HOGGAR
CLAPPING TWO FLAT STONES TOGETHER
A THOUSAND TIMES

1988

CROSSING MARKS

THE SAHARA 1988

SAHARA CIRCLE

1988

DUSTY BOOTS LINE

THE SAHARA 1988

SAHARA LINE

1988

WHERE THE WALK MEETS THE PLACE
A SIX DAY WALK IN THE HOGGAR
THE SAHARA 1988

CLEARING A PATH
A SIX DAY WALK IN THE HOGGAR
THE SAHARA 1988

MIRAGE

A LINE IN THE SAHARA

1988

WHITE BONE
SIGHT
ROCK
YES
THINKING
BURNT
FLIES
BOOTS
HORIZON
ROARING
REDDISH
RELAXED
ANT
GRAVEL
CONE
SYMMETRY
DROPPINGS
FOOTPRINT
SQUINTING
CRUNCHING
SHADOW
VERTEBRAE
CRACKING
TRAIL
KICKING
SAND
BLACK
FLUTTERING
BUZZ
FEATHER
BUTTERFLY
BREATHING
STUMBLE
RHYTHMIC
CLATTERING
DRONE
GLINTING
CREAK
SCRATCH
RIPPLES
PANTING
RIDGE
DRY MOUTH
CRUST
SILHOUETTE
SOFT
WHITE FLOWER
MIDDAY
HOT ROCK
SIDEWIND
ALIGNING
SCATTERED BONES
COBWEB
HAWK
DUSTY
CLOUDLESS
LIZARD
GOAT TRACKS
SIGHING
SHIMMER

HOGGAR HOUR

A SIXTY MINUTE STRAIGHT WALK IN THE SAHARA

1988

A TRAVELLING CIRCLE

A SIX DAY WALK IN THE HOGGAR

THE SAHARA 1988

TOUAREG CIRCLE
THE SAHARA 1988

WIND LINE

A WIND DIRECTION EACH DAY
ALONG A 560 MILE WALK IN 20½ DAYS
FROM THE ATLANTIC COAST TO THE MEDITERRANEAN COAST

PORTUGAL AND SPAIN 1989

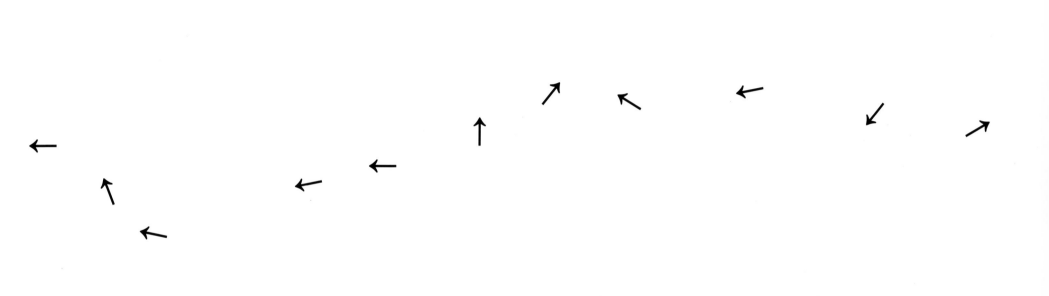

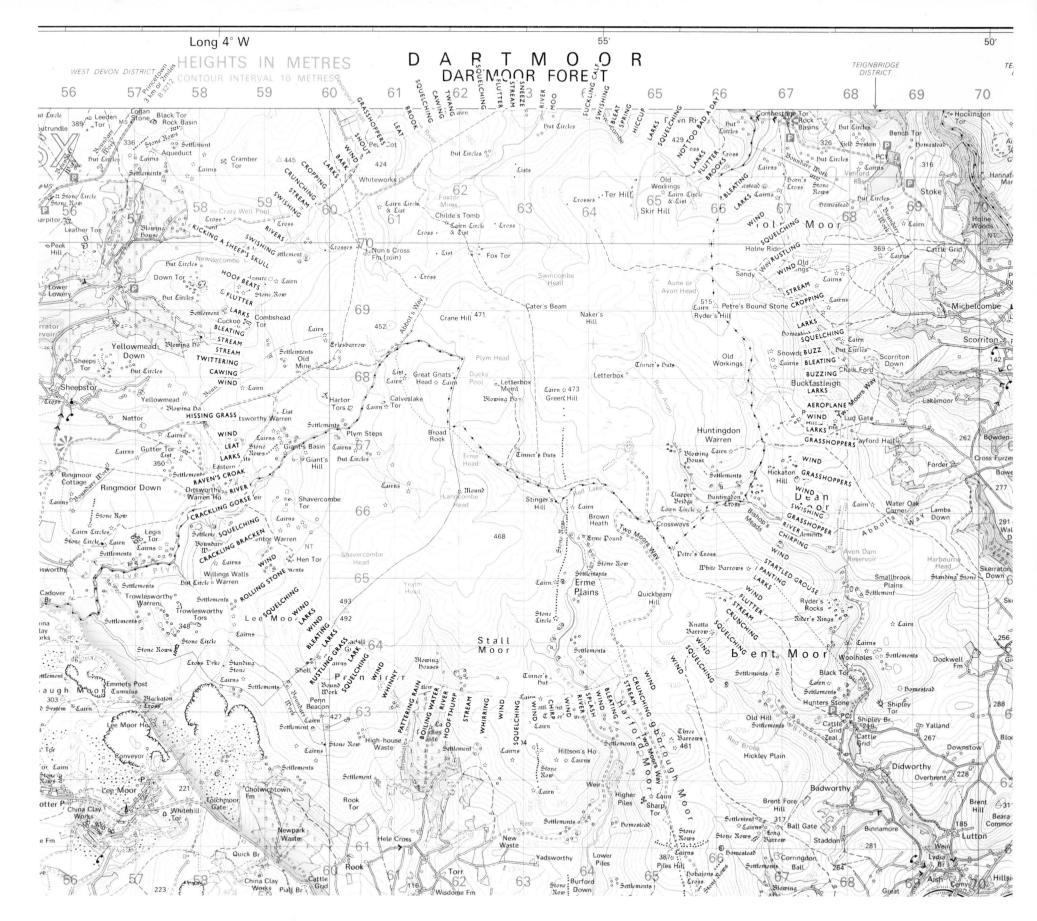

SOUND CIRCLE A WALK ON DARTMOOR 1990

236

HOME CIRCLE

BRISTOL 1989

OLD MUDDY

WELL, THESE ARE THE STRAIGHT FACTS
BUT THEY DON'T COME IN A STRAIGHT LINE.

Roll over Beethoven 1956.
North Face Eiger Direct 1966.
'A LINE MADE BY WALKING ENGLAND 1967.'
First moon walk 1969.

One evening in June 1972, as I was preparing to sleep out for the night near Stonehenge, I saw another traveller arranging his sleeping bag beside a haystack. The following morning was the solstice. Some months later, after a conversation with Richard Long, I deduced he was the solitary figure I had seen, prior to his walk from Stonehenge to Glastonbury.

'ON MIDSUMMER'S DAY A WESTWARD WALK FROM STONEHENGE AT SUNRISE TO GLASTONBURY BY SUNSET FORTY FIVE MILES FOLLOWING THE DAY 1972.'

(Circumference of the earth – measurement of circles – steps of the sun.)

In November 1972, Richard Long and I made a visit to the prehistoric ground drawings in Peru, known as the Nazca Lines, located approximately 250 miles south of Lima.

By chance, we met Maria Reiche, the German mathematician who has devoted her life to the study and preservation of the drawings. Maria Reiche very generously gave us a copy of her booklet, *Mystery on the Desert* (published in Lima, 1949). On page 2, under the heading, 'How the designs were made', she writes: 'A reddish brown, almost black colour characterizes the plains and mountains of this region, which is exceptionally rich in iron. Being produced by oxidation and the effects of thousands of years of daily morning dew followed by excessive heat, this colour does not reach deeper than one or two inches. The stones and gravel underneath are yellowish white. This contrast made it possible to use the level surfaces as immense blackboards on which white designs could be produced on a dark background by simply removing the upper-layer of black stones.'

(The line of sight.
'... make straight paths for your feet ...' Hebrews XII, 13.

Lines of energy – rings, spirals, and straight channels of magnetic current.)

In Tony Morrison's book, *Pathways to the Gods* (1978), he asks whether comparisons could be made between the animal drawings of Nazca and the Zodiac at Glastonbury.

(Dod Lane.)

'Over hill, over dale,
Thorough bush, thorough brier,
Over park, over pale,
Thorough flood, thorough fire ...'

William Shakespeare, *A Midsummer Night's Dream*, Act Two, Scene One.

'A TEN MILE WALK ENGLAND 1968.'

(Unerringly straight line walked on ground – drawn straight line on map.)

(Dartmoor compass tacking.)

February 1981. Richard Long and I made an eleven day walk on the Altiplano of western Bolivia. From General Pérez train station by the Rio Mauri, we walked out to the Rio Achuta, and back to General Pérez. From our turn-around point we could see a snow-capped volcano on the horizon. This was the 6,542 metre high Sajama. Back in England, looking through *Pathways to the Gods*, I read a description by Morrison who made a reconaissance flight over Sajama. 'Lines led in every direction. All of those I could see were single paths and often led unerringly over hills and gullies. All were apparently clear, so either the vegetation had been reduced by recent clearings and walking, or it had never grown over since the paths were made.'

(Nothing hidden.)

On our 1981 visit we had no knowledge of any straight pathways across the Altiplano.

(We-speak-of-what-we-have-seen.)

———————————————

'Why are you doing this?'
'To get to the other side.'
'Do you have a special diet?'
'No, just food and plenty of it.'

Bruce Tulloh, *Four Million Footsteps*, 1970. (A 64 day, 21 hour, 50 minute marathon run across the United States, Los Angeles to New York, 1969.)

'And what sense has the undertaking?'

'That I can't explain. But I am mad enough to contend that above all else the inexplicable gives meaning to life.'

Reinhold Messner, *The Crystal Horizon*, 1989. (The first solo ascent of Mount Everest without the use of artificial oxygen, 1980.)

'It's the going-for-ever-on-ness that I find the attraction.'

Sebastian Snow, *The Rucksack Man*, 1976. (Snow walked 8,700 miles from Tierra del Fuego to Panama City, 1973-4.)

'There are times in life, you can count them in minutes, when you experience an awareness far greater than you usually find in a year.'

F.M. Dostoevsky (quoted in *All 14 Eight Thousanders*, by Reinhold Messner, 1987).

'I noticed how Pete used to make copious entries into a diary, so many that I could not visualize how he could do or say anything without the awareness that he was going to record that action or word. I had found after Dunagiri the value of recording the days as they passed, in order to keep track of time, and I made one-line notes in the form of a diary.'

Joe Tasker, *Savage Arena*, 1982.

'Never write anything. You'll only regret it.'

Don Whillans, 1983 (as quoted in *Thin Air*, by Greg Child, 1988).

YAK-YAK-YAK-NAG-NAG-NAG-YAK-YAK-YAK

('A dog is not reckoned good because he barks well, and a man is not reckoned wise because he speaks skilfully.' Chuang-Tzu.)

Campfire friendship. River water, liquid fuel. Hot tea. Why make walks? To clear the mind, thoughts drifting effortlessly to the surface like tea leaves. Why walk? To make sculpture. Why walk in nature? To attempt a balance of influences. (Quantities of time.) Why walk? Partly to live in 'real time'. In 1975 I made a walk with Richard Long in Nepal. I remember becoming aware of 'foreign topics'. In a sense, the 'foreign topics' were like newspapers – they had nothing to do with the walk. On several of our walks we have had no map for part or all of the walk. No map – no tent – no stove. (No boots, no hair.... Like a rolling stone.) In Nepal in 1983 we travelled for one week on paths without a map, simply asking the way. As our destination found us, I can say in retrospect that everybody we asked gave the appropriate instructions. We lived in 'real time', addicted to walking.

(Escapism - commitment.)

Hinterstoisser Traverse.

'The magic line.' It would be true to say that Richard Long has no real interest in mountain climbing as a sport, but I have chosen to introduce the topic because it is both physical and philosophical in ways that much contemporary sculpture is not.

Why visit Nepal? Jet time is not 'real time'. For the mountaineer it is clear – Wanda Rutkiewicz could not have climbed to 8,611 metres (K-2 summit, Pakistan) in Poland. An artist is free to take up a different position, and only walk on her or his native country. My answer to why visit Nepal would have to be: spiritual influence. (Fly to the other side of the world on a 'hunch'.) To be influenced both by nature and people's lives (who live in nature). As a walking sculptor, Richard Long has been influenced by a wide range of landscapes: Dartmoor (Alaska), Ben Nevis (Kilimanjaro), Alaska (Lappland), riverbeds (riverbanks), Lappland (Dartmoor), Altiplano (Sahara), Silbury Hill (Mulanje Mountain). Any natural location of 'power' demands honesty.

(Twisted ankle and vice versa.)

'Please don't take away my highway shoes.' Bob Dylan.

Boots. Wear them in. Wear them out. Put them on. Take them off. Put them on. (The wrong boots.) The right boots. *The dead boots*. The-boots-without-soul. (As the boots walk, so they stand still, momentarily, with each step.) 'One thing leads to another.' 'Here we go again.' 'So far, so good.' 'Win a few, lose a few.' Familiar phrases can have a new dimension on walks. Often the humour of a popular line has a sense of depth and irony the other Zen classics cannot reach. On a coast to coast road walk, TV's Magnus Magnusson says it all: 'I've started, so I'll finish.'

(Forest fires – unemployment time, employment time – wolves.)

Heathrow and the pre-walk tonsure.

Diary entry: 22 February 1987. Tarahumara, Sierra, Mexico. 'This morning while sitting round the campfire I related to Richard how, when I was a kid, with friends, we used to cook potatoes in my father's wheelbarrow. Gazing silently into the flames for some moments, Richard then said, "Meals on wheels." We laughed. He then continued, "Wheels on fire" (after the C+W song). Laughter. To which I replied: "This me-al will ex-plode."'

Neither overstated nor understated.

An *ordinary* location can be transformed by an *incredible* walk.

'He who knows does not speak, he who speaks does not know.' (Lao Tzu.)

(Heavy as a rock, carrying food. Lighter, weaker.)

'Using a stone for a pillow, I drift towards the clouds.' (Santoka Taneda, Japanese haiku poet, walked 28,000 miles between 1926 and 1940.)

No matter what the length of a walk by Richard Long is, it is appropriate to the art. A few straight muddy feet ('WALKING A LINE IN BORDEAUX 1981'), a handful of miles ('GRANITE STEPPING-STONE CIRCLE. A 5 MILE CIRCULAR WALK ON DARTMOOR PASSING OVER 409 ROCK SLABS AND BOULDERS'), or a thousand mile spiral on England in 1974, kicking off at Bootle near Liverpool. 'Walk a thousand miles, and there is always a beyond...' A short walk is not a short walk that should've been a long walk, not short

because of a lack of stamina or an excess of alcohol. (The body determines thoughts.)

(British Rail regrets to announce the late arrival of ...)

'I'm growing tired of the big city lights,
tired of the glamour and tired of the sights,
in all my dreams I am roaming once more,
back to my home on the old river shore...'

'Miss the Mississippi and you', as sung by Jimmie Rodgers, the singing brakeman.

(River Avon dreaming – clear mind, 'muddy waters'.)

SNAKES (CAPITALISM) WORMS (SOCIALISM) RATS (WEALTH) LICE (POVERTY) RAIN (HOMELESSNESS).

Diary entry: 9 July 1984. Ladakh, India. 'Set off at six walked up to the ravine, followed it up till it obviously was not the route. Back down to the main river then back downstream to a cairn and small track, no track up scree slope – this also no good. Back down to the main river then upstream arriving at correct river fork at 15.00 in the rain. Feeling slow on the path up towards the pass – but too wet and tired, back down again to the 15.00 stop. Now under a rock overhang. We have no idea how it will go, a problem to solve: time and distance, river conditions, rain, visibility. A cold damp night – mind uncertain.' H.F.

'Uncertain the journey's end, our destination; uncertain too, the place from whence we come.' (Noh play, Japan.)

Crossroads – river crossings. Rivers are roads that move.

Decisions, decisions. Walking is all about decisions, unfolding and (very carefully) folding the map. (Retracing, through the rain-soaked, disintegrating folds.) In the art of Richard Long there are two areas of interrelated decisions – the sculpture and the walk. (Walk works. I grew up in Newcastle, and of that city, Wilfred Pickles once commented, 'It's the only place where people work to wak, instead of wakin' to work.') When I see an exhibition of Richard Long's art I savour what I imagine were the decisions, some ideas even causing me to laugh, in appreciation. For instance, the 1980 150 mile walk home. ('Hello. I am a Dutch art student. Please may I make a plaster cast of your doorstep?') From Totnes to Bristol. First day walked ten miles, second day twenty miles, third day thirty miles, fourth day forty miles, fifth day fifty miles. Strong idea followed by a strong walk – words after the fact. (Unlike the mountaineer who learns from her or his peer group, Richard Long has acquired his walking abilities alone.)

Event as object – distance no object.

Dusty Torma.

Where do you *construct* your art? In a *studio*? Where do you 'spend' most of your time? Twelve days on foot crossing twelve mountain passes in Ladakh...or touring the country for weeks on buses?

(Standing stones – a journey into stillness.)

'Adopt the pace of nature: her secret is patience.' R.W. Emerson.

Circling and drifting
la-te-ral thinking

Canyons of your mind –
and those circles in the corn.

'Our local shopping mall now has a club of people who go "mall-walking" every day. They circle the shopping centre *en masse* – Caldor to Sears to J.C. Penney, circuit after circuit, with an occasional break to shop.'

Bill McKibben, *The End of Nature*, 1990.

Belgium, July 1986. Georges Holtyzer walked 418.49 continuous miles in six days, ten hours and fifty-eight minutes (452 laps of a 1.49 km. circuit). He kept moving for 98.78 per cent of the time (*Guinness Book of Records*).

Neutral wordless distance.

Corduroy Road.

Of the sculptures I have had the pleasure to see on walks, I remember two stunning 'lines'. Wandering over a ridge on the Bolivian Altiplano (1981), I glimpsed, out of the corner of my eye, a line in the distance that flashed at right angles. Becoming unaligned, it was lost amongst the scattered stones and animal tracks. The second line was in Mexico, 1987. An Indian path. By pouring river water from a plastic bottle onto the existing path, Richard Long emphasized several feet of its inherent straightness. The wet, visible line eventually disappearing under a light flurry of snow, melting through momentarily. Walking away, looking back – swirling snow, rocks, and pine trees – the line now existing only in my memory. Sweat on the boots.

'Imagine,
  No more sculpture
  No more Henry Moore...'

From the Roger Ackling version of 'Imagine' by John Lennon.

'Nothing is so precious that we cannot afford to throw it away.'
Jacks, *Religious Perplexities*.

The Strand ley line:
St. Martin-in-the-Fields.
St. Mary-le-Strand.
St. Clement Danes.
St. Dunstan-in-the-West.
Arnold Circus.

Sometime in the late 1960s, I remember walking through London's crowded streets with Richard Long. We discussed the possibility of seeing someone who had walked to Oxford Street (a figure in the crowd) from the port of Dover, having taken the ferry from Calais. The point of this story is that the hypothetical traveller had walked to Calais from Vladivostock in the eastern U.S.S.R.

(Corina Corina – mud on the tracks – blood on the socks.)

The early sculptures of Richard Long had a strong impact on me. Disarming simplicity – a whole new way of thinking (since childhood). Lightness – contemporary art with no history. This year (1990), I clapped eyes on a new work that immediately reminded me of the student days, the sixties' sculptures. In the small back room of a London gallery was a powerful work (Dragon), embodying that unique sense of risk – spirit – nature. A small zigzag line of white china clay splashed across the clean floor (go with the flow – earth's gravity).

(The wave: walk water sculpture sleep – walk water sculpture sleep – walk water sculpture sleep.)

STONED.

No Monday Morning Blues. Today it might be easy to criticize Richard Long's success, but it must not be forgotten that after leaving St. Martin's School of Art he did not look for a job. He made sculpture. ('Instead of earning a wage, you are earning mountain experience.' Dougal Haston, *In High Places*, 1972.)

'Crossing the Ohio at Louisville, I steered through the big city by compass without speaking a word to anyone.'

September 2nd 1867. John Muir, *A Thousand Mile Walk to the Gulf*.

About one hundred years later Richard Long created 'A LINE MADE BY WALKING ENGLAND 1967', surely one of the most original works of twentieth-century western art. ('The longest journey begins with but a single step.') At the age of twenty-three, Long combined two seemingly unrelated activities: sculpture (the line) and walking (the action). A line (made by) walking. In time, the sculpture will have disappeared, long before the commercialization of the word 'green'... and those footprints on the moon.

'Leave no turd unstoned.'

Don Whillans, 1983, as quoted in *Thin Air*, by Greg Child, 1988.

As Britain's *premier* sculptor, Richard Long has not been tempted into making U-turns (except for his walk, crossing and recrossing England and Wales, 'CROSSING STONES 1987'). Fame and fortune have not caused him to employ bulldozers after a lifetime of 'placing' sticks. Long makes a variety of work – enough for four artists, but they are related, one to another. This variety is not so diverse as to be hypocritical. We are not confused as to his real concerns. Rain, snow, sleet, and ice eventually form the same river.

Calumniare Fortiter,
Et Aliquid Adhaerebit.
(Throw dirt enough, and some will stick.)

(River mud – hand of the artist – life line – the all-meaning circle – Lascaux.)

Feng-shui (wind and water) Chernobyl.
Six months before 26 April 1986, Richard Long and I drank river water, flow-

ing through the land of the Lapps. A fifteen day walk of wind, rain, freezing rain, snow, blizzard, and friendship.

(Shigechiyo Izumi. Japanese. Born 29 June 1865. Lived for 120 years and 237 days.)

Length of a stride – length of a life.

Spain, February 1989. Walking down a snaking road through pine trees, I was reminded of the *Tour de France* cycle race. Richard Long and I had set out to walk coast to coast across Portugal and Spain. For the record, the walking artist walks every step of the way, whereas in recent years the *Tour* cyclists have been flown between two stages, creating a gap in the chain of roads. Similarly, in 1974, the Scottish hill-walker, H.Brown, made a walk billed as the first non-stop climb of all the 3,000 foot Scottish Munro peaks. On the road-links between the hills, Brown in fact travelled by bicycle. Inevitably, Richard Long and I began to talk of the English racer Tommy Simpson. We recalled the view on film of Simpson in the 1967 *Tour*, falling from his cycle, to die where he fell, on the road. Our short conversation then switched to the American, Greg LeMond, who at the time of our walk had won the 1986 *Tour*. After an incredible recovery following a shooting accident, LeMond went on to win a second *Tour* in July 1989. (Teaching by example.)

(On the road.)

In the late summer of 1989, I made a coast to coast road walk across France. From west to east, my route developed daily. One particular day I remember well. On the dawn of October 5th, while descending Mont Ventoux, by chance I came across the roadside memorial to Tommy Simpson. A plaque and a cairn of cyclists' caps.

(Dartmoor renewal.)

BASHOBECKETTBARTHES – LEMOND?

I do not mention the *Tour de France* to glorify a competitive way of life. The truth is, I find the three-time winner of the *Tour de France* an inspiration: LeMond has passed-through-the-eye-of-a-needle. These events are the landmarks of his life. This is magic.

Richard Long makes his marks....This is magic.

It has been my great privilege to make ten journeys with Richard Long, and I thank him.

Hamish Fulton   Summer 1990

Footnote. December 1990.

Dream walk. Eleventh journey. This winter, Richard Long and I walked on 622 miles of roads from the north coast to the south coast of Spain – Ribadesella to Málaga, crossing our previous west to east route in the town of Villanueva. 'Whoso shall compel thee to go one mile, go with them twain.' DOS MAS. On the road to Las Hazuelas, the bottom line –

THE REALITY

OF THE LOCALITY

AN INTERVIEW WITH RICHARD LONG BY RICHARD CORK

RC Your exhibitions demonstrate that you know exactly how to handle gallery space with the spare lucidity which characterizes your outdoor work. But of course remote country is a very different arena from a gallery. So how do you go about re-creating the outdoor experience indoors?

RL In the way that the photographs and texts feed the imagination. The sculptures that you can see directly in the gallery feed the senses, and also the mud works which are made directly on the wall. I like to present art in a very concrete way in a gallery, as well as presenting images from remote places. I think also the photographs have the function that I can make a piece of work, for example, in a canyon in Mexico, by pouring water down a rock face to make a water drawing, and then record that idea and bring it back into the world of art. Photographs are useful for recording a work which may only last for the time that the water drawing dries in the sunshine.

RC Do you find it easier to work outdoors than in a gallery context?

RL I enjoy both ways of working, and for me it is necessary to use both possibilities. I think if I only worked outdoors it could perhaps be seen as romantic escapism.

RC Do you ever wish that the gallery visitor could actually see your work in the landscape?

RL All the places where I make my work, such as the Highlands, or on Dartmoor, are free public places where anyone can go. So it is quite possible that people can go to the locations of my walks and often the information is provided, as in the map works. It is not my intention that they should actually repeat the walks, because not only do they belong to a certain place, but they also belong to a certain time. You can never repeat the time but certainly people can go to the places of my walks. Also, it is not true to think that my landscape sculptures are never seen. They are sometimes seen by local people in the country, occasionally as I make them, or discovered by chance by people who might not recognize them as art but who would nevertheless see them. I am sort of interested in all the different contexts that work can be put into the world and then also received back by different people in different circumstances.

RC But it is surely significant that you would never, by choice, make your work outdoors with people looking on while you were doing it.

RL No, it is never a performance. It is usually a very private, quiet activity. I am happy to make it in solitude. I think part of the energy in my work is that I have the opportunity to make art in amazing, beautiful landscapes which are very strong and powerful. Somehow part of the power and the energy comes from being alone in that place. The simplicity and feeling of being alone is actually part of the work. So it would be quite inappropriate to have a load of people visiting it at a particular site, as that would change the whole nature of the place. So I think that is another way my photographs work. They present the idea that art can be made in solitude or in very remote places, or lasts for very few minutes, or be seen by very few people, or be seen by people from a different culture.

RC How much of the year on average do you spend walking, would you say?

RL It is difficult to say. I have never measured it, but probably not more than half. I don't consider myself a nomad, and I am not a person who is endlessly wandering. I like to go to places for a certain reason, following a certain idea, and to do a piece of work which lasts for a certain amount of time. Then when I have finished that work I always like to come home. So it is a necessary part of my life to be quiet at home in Bristol. That is also part of the way I like to live. I think if I was travelling all the time I would not have the right type of energy to start making a big walk. It is necessary to have an appetite. Often a good walk comes after spending a month or so in Bristol, just answering letters and doing paperwork. Then I have a good appetite to go out into the landscape.

RC Since you also spend a lot of time holding exhibitions all over the world, you must be a highly organized person.

RL Well, I think to be a professional full-time artist it is necessary to be very organized. I think, like a lot of artists, the most organized thing you see about me is my work. So probably the work is more organized than my life.

RC How do you decide where to take the next walk?

RL Oh, for a variety of reasons. I like the idea that it is possible to go around to the other side of the world almost on a hunch. I may have a feeling or an idea that some place might be interesting, or I may never have been there before, or know nothing about it. That is a good enough reason to find out what that place is like.

RC So you don't necessarily research a place before you go there?

RL Well, it depends. There are certain walks close to home, like a piece I did this summer in Scotland where I had a particular idea about making a walk in the Highlands. Because you can get good maps in Britain it was possible to plan the walk by looking at maps; I could know the place in advance. So then, it was just a question of going to the place and carrying out the walk. In other places, like the Hoggar mountains in the Sahara where I went this year, it is not possible to get good maps. So you have a completely different way of going about walking. The way I found my way in the Sahara was just by following the places where I could get water, without using a map. So some walks are with maps and some without.

RC Do you ever get lost?

RL There are different ways of getting lost, but not fundamentally lost. Sometimes just for a couple of hours here and there in a mist. In the early days, when I used to make straight walks across Dartmoor, one of the things I used to like about walking in a straight line was that, apart from the intellectual beauty of a straight line, it is the most practical way to cross a moor. No matter what the weather is doing, and it can be a very thick mist, because I am following a compass line I can do that walk in any conditions and not get lost. So walking by compass in straight lines, apart from anything else, is a very practical part of my work. I think basically all my work is very practical. The only reason I could do the walk in the Sahara was that I had the amazing good luck that before I went there, there happened to be some freak storms that left pools of water in the mountains. Those storms determined that I could walk there, and where I could find water determined the shape of the walk. So, in fact, how it turned out was that the walk lasted for six days. Each day the little pools of water were drying up and disappearing into the ground. So at the end of the six days the water had disap-

peared, and that is when the walk ended. So it had a nice kind of practical logic about it.

RC What do you actually think about when you are on your own and walking, mile after mile, in often quite deserted territory?

RL Well, you can think about everything. I think all I can say is that somehow having the rhythmic relaxation of walking many hours each day puts me into a state of mind which frees the imagination. Quite often I get ideas for new works by doing a walk. In other words one walk leads to another.

RC So you never feel lonely?

RL Oh, no. It never occurs to me to feel lonely. I just think I am very lucky to have these pockets of freedom and silence, escaping from the normal chaos of everyday life in the art world. It is like another dimension I can have in my life.

RC Do you find some landscapes are more conducive to work than others?

RL Oh, yes. I would say that for a start, the British landscape is interesting. It is my home landscape, and I find it very rich. Even the footpaths and lanes of the West Country, and then the moorlands and the Highlands. The moorlands in Britain are interesting - it is a very particular type of landscape. Ireland is another country which I feel very sympathetic to. I have very strong feelings about it because basically, in the west, it is my type of landscape, a sort of stony, wet desert, also with a lot of nice people and a lot of humour and beautiful music. So that is another interesting country. I would also say that Bolivia is again another big, stony desert. I think in a strange way that landscapes like the Tundra, like Alaska for example - it's almost like being on Dartmoor but it is much bigger. So in a way I often feel at home in places like Lappland or Alaska because their boggy, windy, flattish kind of landscape is sort of familiar to me. I think there are certain things that are fairly universal. Footpaths interest me a lot, and you could almost say that the footpath going up Ben Nevis is more or less the same as all the great footpaths in Nepal. It is just that in Nepal the views on either side are bigger and higher and the precipices on each side are much bigger, but basically a footpath is a footpath and it is probably the same in China as in Scotland. It is just one stone after another. It is like a walk, just one footstep after another no matter where it is. So I am interested in homing in on the universal similarities between things, but also on the great differences between places, because each place on the earth is absolutely unique, and no stone is like another stone in that respect. I am all for using that as well.

RC Do you mind bad weather, or extremes of heat or cold?

RL Oh, no. I think being a sort of typical British walker, being used to the pouring rain, I'm not bothered about getting wet, and I utterly love all the different types of weather. I just take the world as I find it really. I suppose that I would say that I have been in cold, wet, temperate climates more than very hot climates. But that is more to do with the fact that to make walks alone and to be independent I always have to be near water. So, apart from this last strange occasion in the Sahara, I would not go to a place where it was so dry that I couldn't find water, as I cannot carry water with me.

RC How do you decide when to stop walking and make a work?

RL Well, when I come to an incredible place I don't have to make that decision. I have an instantaneous feeling that this is the place and here are the stones and I just get on with it.

RC Then it is absolutely a question of taking your cue from the place that you find?

RL Oh, yes. But that is not to say that certain sculptures can't be pre-planned. Again, it is a combination of things. For instance, in Ladakh, in the mountains of Kashmir, on the last trip I made there, by walking on the footpaths after a few days I had the idea to make actual walking lines on the footpath. That is an example of having an idea after a few days of being on the walk. The actual walking and the footpaths give me the idea to make the work. When I was by some strange circumstances in Alaska, I happened to find myself on the Arctic Circle, and it seemed just the perfect opportunity and place for me to make a circle. Sometimes it might happen that I have the idea to make a circle or something and then the actual place will - like in Africa, I was going to make a circle of stones on a high mountain in Malaŵi and then, when I got there, I couldn't find any stones because there was no ice and snow to break the rock up. So I kept the idea of a circle and changed the material to burnt cacti which were lying around, that had been burnt in lightning storms. That is just to show how I can keep one half of the idea and then change the other half because of the circumstances of the place. I am an opportunist; I just take advantage of the places and situations I find myself in.

RC There is still a contrast, though, between what you describe as the opportunism of responding to a particular place that you didn't previously know about, and the unwavering constancy of the language that you always favour - the lines and the circles.

RL Yes, it is always like a balance - a harmony of complementary ideas. You could say that my work is also a balance between the patterns of nature and the formalism of human, abstract ideas like lines and circles. It is where my human characteristics meet the natural forces and patterns of the world, and that is really the kind of subject of my work.

RC Since they play such an important role in the form assumed by your work, can you say something more about why you favour lines and circles as such?

RL Well, I have to say that the first time I used a circle I had no idea why I used it. It seemed like a good idea at the time, but having made it, it looked great and seemed a very strong and powerful image, and I have used it ever since. There are a lot of things theoretical and intellectual to say about lines and circles, but I think the very fact that they are images that don't belong to me and, in fact, are shared by everyone because they have existed throughout history, actually makes them more powerful than if I was inventing my own idiosyncratic, particular Richard Long-type images. I think it cuts out a lot of personal unwanted aesthetic paraphernalia.

RC They give you freedom, in other words.

RL Yes, that is right. In fact, they actually allow me to home in on other things, so the circles stay the same in the different places I make them around the world but the places change. It means that the viewer of my work is noticing that there are circles, but he is also seeing that the places are changing and the materials are changing. I think, anyway, a circle is such an open system and that it can be a vehicle for perhaps any idea under the sun. It is a freedom, as you say. I can make a circle of words, I can make a circle of stones, I can make a circle of mud with my hands on a wall, I can walk in a circle for one hundred miles. It is a completely adaptable image and form and system.

RC Yes, you can make full circles, empty circles, circles with upright stones, circles with horizontal stones.

RL And it is also an image that everyone recognizes. So people don't actually have to fathom out what they are looking at.

RC You are aiming then, in essence, at universality.

RL Yes, but I think nature is universal. It is no coincidence that there are parallels between my work and work from certain people of other cultures and societies, as nature, which is the source of my work, is universal. We all live in different cultures but we all share the same nature of the world. We all share the same air, the same water and everything.

RC When I see lines in your work, they often remind me of the fact that duration is involved, that walking is fundamental and that a journey is being undertaken. You have always been strikingly preoccupied with movement, distance and time.

RL Yes, time is the fourth dimension in my work, and I am interested in using it in a very particular way. So I have made walks about pace, walks about time only, and also certain geometries, for example, walking between a hundred Tors on Dartmoor in a hundred hours, or walking a thousand miles in a thousand hours. So it is possible to use time almost in a very classical way, as a very formal, geometric thing.

RC Why is walking so central a part of your work? Does the act of walking make you experience time more vividly than you would do in normal life?

RL Yes, I think it does. Like art itself, it is like a focus. It gets rid of a lot of things and you can actually concentrate. So getting myself into these solitary days of repetitive walking or in empty landscapes is just a certain way of emptying out or simplifying my life, just for those few days or weeks, into a fairly simple but concentrated activity which, as you say, is really quite different from the way that people normally live their lives, which is very complicated. So my art is a simplification. Also, a walk is a great vehicle for very particular ideas, about colours, trees, time, anything I choose.

RC Does time pass more slowly for you during a walk, or more quickly?

RL Ah, well, it plays funny tricks doesn't it, time. It is both. I would say it is very curious that if I am doing a long walk, at the beginning the number of days ahead seem a lot, and it seems like a long way to the end of the walk! After about three-quarters of the way through, it seems that the completed days have just flashed by, so time is completely subjective, or relative. There is no real time.

RC While you are making the work in the landscape, what state of mind do you like to be in, or do you find yourself in?

RL Well, usually I am happy and relaxed. I would say that the way I make my work is from the things that give me pleasure and the materials that I like using - my work doesn't come from a kind of *angst* or discontent. A sculpture in a landscape, when it really happens well in a good way, is like a celebration of the place and my feelings of me being there and having the right idea at the right time and everything coming together in a good way. For me that is the perfect way to make a good work. But I can be happy like that in a gallery making a big mud work on a wall or something. Part of the pleasure actually comes from the physical side of things. It is very important for me to make my work, you know, the actual physical making - standing the stones up, the long walking, the physical toil, the sweating and the getting tired, or the getting covered in mud in a gallery throwing mud around a circle. I would say that as well as my work being about ideas, it is also about that physical enjoyment.

RC Do you think that in order perhaps to engage your mind and your imagination fully you have to involve the whole of your body as well?

RL Oh, yes. The work is the expression of both the intellect and the body, they are absolutely complementary. It is no good just having a good idea, it is also necessary for me to make it, and also not have somebody else make it - for me to do it myself, because my work is my own footsteps, it is only what I can do, so the handprints in the gallery are my hands and the stones that I turn up on the mountainside are the stones that I can physically handle myself at that place. And I have found that place by walking to it. My work is a portrait of myself in the world, my own personal journey through it and the materials that I find along the way.

RC Watching the film that Philip Haas recently made about your work, I was very struck by the amount of physical exertion - the amount of sheer hard work, if you like - involved in making some of these big stone pieces.

RL Well, it is not hard work because I enjoy it, but anyway it is work.

RC And you must feel fairly tired afterwards.

RL Yes, but it is a nice kind of tiredness.

RC And then you take a photograph of the work. How do you go about that?

RL Well, normally I just step back and point the camera and try and get it in focus. Even though it is necessary to get a good photograph, the photographs should be as simple as possible so that when people look at the photograph they are not dazzled by wide-angled lenses or special effects. Because my art is very simple and straightforward, I think the photographs have got to be fairly simple and straightforward, so that the feeling of the work somehow accurately comes through. That is why most of the photographs are taken from my eye level. Usually, after I have made the work, I kind of walk around it and somehow find the best place to take the photograph. A line usually has the characteristic of pointing out of or beyond itself, maybe to the horizon, so often the alignment of the viewer, the line and something a long way off is important. Circles are different, they are more enclosed, more of a stopping place.

RC Let me end by asking probably the most important and difficult question which arises from your work. Why do you think that you do go out to these remote places again and again? Is it bound up with establishing and developing an increasingly close relationship with nature?

RL I have no idea really. I have never had any ideology or fixed ideas. I think all that has happened is that my first landscape works were made in and around Bristol. My first turf works were actually made in my parents' front garden. As I have got older and I have had the wherewithal to extend my arena of making work, it has just got wider and wider, so that finally I have made works in different countries and landscapes around the world.

RC But I want to press you a bit further on this. What do you think you gain from this closeness with the natural world?

RL I think it is just the choice that I have made for myself. I do the things that have a deep meaning for me. I have the most sublime or profound feelings when I am walking, or touching natural materials in natural places. That is what I've decided to do and that is what I am showing you in my art.

RC Since so much of the finest art produced in this country has revolved around an intense response to landscape, do you feel close to any British tradition in this wish to commune with nature?

RL No, not particularly. Just by being English, in my childhood, having my grandparents living on Dartmoor, in Devon, or going on cycling holidays with my father when I was a boy. I think all those things were much more important than this so-called tradition of English landscape art. I realize there was a sort of romantic movement as a result of the industrial revolution. I suppose if you have to put some historical or political slant on my work, I hope it does tie up in some ways with the Green philosophy, 'small is beautiful', and of seeing the world as one place, and using its raw materials with respect. I like to see art as being a return to the senses.

Broadcast in 'Third Ear', BBC Radio 3, Friday 28 October 1988. Produced by Judith Bumpus.

Richard Long was born in Bristol, England, in 1945. He studied at the West of England College of Art, Bristol, from 1962 to 1965 and at St.Martin's School of Art, London, from 1966 to 1968. On 14 October 1988 he was awarded the *Kunstpreis Aachen, Neue Galerie – Sammlung Ludwig*; in November 1989 the Turner Prize, Tate Gallery, London; and on 15 June 1990 was named *Chevalier dans l'Ordre des Arts et des Lettres* by the French Government. Richard Long lives and works in Bristol.

ONE-MAN EXHIBITIONS

1968
Düsseldorf, Galerie Konrad Fischer, *Richard J. Long: Sculpture*, 21 September – 18 October.

1969
New York, John Gibson Gallery, *Richard Long*, 22 February - 14 March.
Düsseldorf, Galerie Konrad Fischer, *Richard J. Long*, 5 July – 1 August.
Krefeld, Museum Haus Lange, *Richard Long Exhibition One Year*, July 1969 – 1970. Catalogue, in German and English, with text by Paul Wember, published at end of exhibition as "Richard Long Land Art im Museum Haus Lange Krefeld".
Paris, Galerie Yvon Lambert, *Richard Long - Sculpture*, 5 – 26 November.
Milan, Galerie Lambert, *A Sculpture by Richard Long*, 15 November – 1 December.

1970
Düsseldorf, Galerie Konrad Fischer, *Eine Skulptur von Richard Long*, 11 May – 9 June.
Mönchengladbach, Städtisches Museum Mönchengladbach, *Richard Long: 4 Sculptures*, 16 July – 30 August (see Publications).
New York, Dwan Gallery, *Richard Long*, 3 – 29 October.

1971
Turin, Gian Enzo Sperone, *Richard Long*, April.
Amsterdam, Art & Project, *Richard Long*, 17 July – 6 August.
London, Whitechapel Art Gallery, *Richard Long*, 9 – 21 November.

Oxford, Museum of Modern Art, *Richard Long*, 9 – 23 December.

1972
New York, The Museum of Modern Art, *"Projects": Richard Long*, 14 March – 17 April (in collaboration with The British Council).
Paris, Galerie Yvon Lambert, *Richard Long: Look the Ground in the Eye*, opened 3 May.

1973
London, Lisson Gallery, *Richard Long*, 23 January – 24 February.
Antwerp, Wide White Space, *Richard Long*, 15 March – 12 April.
Düsseldorf, Galerie Konrad Fischer, *Richard Long: A rolling stone*, 29 May – 25 June.
Amsterdam, Stedelijk Museum, *Richard Long*, 7 December 1973 – 27 January 1974 (see Publications).

1974
New York, John Weber Gallery, *Richard Long*, 4 – 29 May.
Edinburgh, Scottish National Gallery of Modern Art, *Richard Long*, 19 July – 11 August (see Publications).
London, Lisson Gallery, *Richard Long*, 1 – 30 November.
Düsseldorf, Galerie Konrad Fischer, *Richard Long*, 20 December 1974 – 19 January 1975.

1975
Amsterdam, Art & Project, *Richard Long: River Avon Driftwood; Crossing two Rivers/Minnesota/Wiltshire*, 18 March – 5 April.
Antwerp, Wide White Space, *Richard Long: Driftwood*, 15 April – 16 May.
Paris, Galerie Yvon Lambert, *Richard Long*, 24 April – 20 May.
Basle, Galerie Rolf Preisig, *Richard Long*, 12 June – 12 July.
Plymouth, Plymouth School of Art, *Richard Long*.

1976
Rome, Gian Enzo Sperone, *Richard Long*, 16 March – April.
Düsseldorf, Galerie Konrad Fischer, *Richard Long*, 15 May – 11 June.
Antwerp, Wide White Space, *Richard Long*, 25 May – 10 June.

London, Lisson Gallery, *Richard Long: Stones*, 24, 25, 26 June.
Venice, XXXVII Venice Biennale 1976, British Pavilion, *Richard Long*, 18 July – 10 October. Catalogue with text by Michael Compton.
Bristol, Arnolfini, *Richard Long: River Avon Driftwood*, 16 November – 24 December.
New York, Sperone Westwater Fischer, *Richard Long*, 4 December 1976 – 8 January 1977.
Tokyo, Art Agency Co., Ltd., *Richard Long*.

1977
London, Whitechapel Art Gallery, *Richard Long*, 25 January - 27 February (see Publications).
Amsterdam, Art & Project, *Richard Long*, 8 February – 5 March. *Art & Project bulletin 99*.
Poznan, Gallery Akumalatory, *Richard Long*, 9 May – 19 June.
Basle, Galerie Rolf Preisig, *Richard Long*, 17 May – 21 June.
London, Lisson Gallery, *Richard Long*, 21 May – 18 June.
Berne, Kunsthalle, *Richard Long*, 15 July – 7 August (see Publications).
Melbourne, National Gallery of Victoria, *Richard Long*, 8 December 1977 – week ending 7 January 1978 (part of John Kaldor Art Project 6).
Sydney, Art Gallery of New South Wales, *Richard Long: John Kaldor Art Project 6*, 16 December 1977 – 5 February 1978 (see Publications).

1978
Amsterdam, Art & Project, *Richard Long: Driftwood Circle*, 10 January – 4 February.
Paris, Galerie Yvon Lambert, *Richard Long*, 2 February – 3 April.
Düsseldorf, Galerie Konrad Fischer, *Richard Long*, 11 March – 7 April.
London, Lisson Gallery, *Richard Long: Outback*, 2 – 20 May.
Zürich, InK: Halle für internationale neue Kunst, *Richard Long*, 19 July – 31 August.
New York, Sperone Westwater Fischer, *Richard Long*, 30 September – 21 October.
Hamburg, Austellungsraum Ulrich Rückriem, *Richard Long*.
Leeds, Park Square Gallery, *Richard Long*.

1979
Zürich, InK: Halle für internationale neue Kunst, *Richard Long*, 19 February – 8 April.
London, Anthony d'Offay Gallery, *Richard Long: The River Avon*, 15 March – 12 April (see Publications).
Basle, Galerie Rolf Preisig, *Richard Long*, 6 April – 5 May.
Londonderry, The Orchard Gallery, *Recent Work by Richard Long*, 1 – 19 May.
Southampton, University of Southampton, University Gallery, *Richard Long: Chalk Stone Line 1979*, 11 – 29 June.
Eindhoven, Van Abbemuseum, *Richard Long: Sculpturen en Fotowerken*, 29 September – 28 October; travelled, with the addition of one work, to Museum of Modern Art, Oxford, 11 November – 23 December (see Publications).
London, Lisson Gallery, *Richard Long*, 9 October – 9 November.
Tokyo, Art Agency Co., Ltd., *Richard Long*, 20 October – 16 November.

1980
Athens, Karen & Jean Bernier, *Richard Long: Stone Circles*, 1 – 29 March.
Amsterdam, Art & Project, *Richard Long: Stones and Sticks*, 22 March – 19 April. *Art & Project bulletin 116.*
Cambridge, Massachusetts, Fogg Art Museum, Harvard University, *Richard Long*, 17 April – 1 June. Brochure with text by Gabriella Jeppson.
New York, Sperone Westwater Fischer, *Richard Long*, 26 April – 17 May.
London, Anthony d'Offay Gallery, *Richard Long: New Work*, 17 September – 16 October (see Publications).
Düsseldorf, Galerie Konrad Fischer, *Richard Long*, 8 – 29 November.

1981
New York, Sperone Westwater Fischer, *Richard Long*, 10 – 31 January.
Edinburgh, Graeme Murray Gallery, *Richard Long*, 7 – 28 February.
Zürich, Galerie Konrad Fischer, *Richard Long*, 8 May – 6 June.
London, Anthony d'Offay Gallery, *Richard Long*, 3 June – 8 July (see Publications).
Toronto, David Bellman Gallery, *Richard Long: New work*, 12 September – 10 October.

Bordeaux, Centre d'Arts Plastiques Contemporains de Bordeaux, *Richard Long*, 4 December 1981 – 30 January 1982 (see Publications).

1982
Amsterdam, Art & Project, *Richard Long*, 23 January – 20 February. *Art & Project bulletin 128.*
Paris, Galerie Yvon Lambert, *Richard Long*, 13 February – 12 March.
Venice, California, Flow Ace Gallery, *Richard Long*, 1 – 31 May.
New York, Sperone Westwater Fischer, *Richard Long*, 25 September – 23 October.
Ottawa, National Gallery of Canada, *Richard Long*, 21 October 1982 – 9 January 1983. Brochure, in English and French, with text by Jessica Bradley (also see Publications).

1983
Toronto, David Bellman Gallery, *Richard Long: Canadian Sculptures*, 19 March – 16 April.
Bristol, Arnolfini, *Richard Long: Selected Works 1965 – 1983*, 26 March – 7 May (see Publications).
London, Anthony d'Offay Gallery, *Richard Long: New Works*, 29 March – 12 May.
Tokyo, Century Cultural Center, *Richard Long Exhibition*, 18 April – May (see Publications).
Tokyo, Art Agency Tokyo, *Richard Long*, 20 April – 31 May.
Turin, Antonio Tucci Russo, *Richard Long*, 20 May – 30 September (see Publications).
Düsseldorf, Galerie Konrad Fischer, *Richard Long*, 16 September – 14 October.

1984
London, Coracle Press, *Richard Long: Watermarks*, 7 – 31 January.
Naples, Lucio Amelio, *Richard Long: Stone*, 14 January – 6 February.
Paris, Galerie Crousel-Hussenot, *Richard Long: New Works*, 10 March – 15 April.
Athens, Jean Bernier, *Richard Long*, 29 March – 28 April.
Dallas, Dallas Museum of Art, *Concentrations 9: Richard Long*, 31 March – 20 April. Brochure with text by Sue Graze and reprint of artist's statement in *Touchstones* (see Publications).

New York, Sperone Westwater, *Richard Long*, 5 May – 2 June.
Kilkenny, Butler Gallery, Kilkenny Castle, *Richard Long*, 25 August – 23 September.
Londonderry, Orchard Gallery, *Richard Long*, 23 September – 13 October (see Publications).
London, Anthony d'Offay Gallery, *Richard Long*, 16 October – 16 November (see Publications).
Düsseldorf, Galerie Konrad Fischer, *Richard Long*, opened 20 October (duration approximately one month).

1985
Basle, Galerie Buchmann, *Richard Long*, 26 January – 9 March. Book by Armin Wildermuth, *Richard Long und die Nähe der Dinge*.
London, Anthony d'Offay Gallery, *Richard Long: From Pass to Pass*, 4 – 29 June.
Kendal, Abbot Hall Art Gallery, *Richard Long*, 6 July – 1 September. Brochure by Richard Long.
Malmö, Malmö Konsthall, *Richard Long*, 20 September – 13 October and 26 October – 24 November. Poster/brochure, in Swedish, with text by Sune Nordgren.
Milan, Padiglione d'Arte Contemporanea di Milano, *Il Luogo Buono: Richard Long*, 29 November 1985 – 25 February 1986 (see Publications).

1986
Madrid, Palacio de Cristal, *Piedras: Richard Long*, 28 January – 20 April (see Publications).
Paris, Galerie Crousel-Hussenot, *Richard Long: Oeuvres Recentes*, 12 April – 13 May.
New York, Sperone Westwater, *Richard Long*, 6 – 16 September.
New York, The Solomon R. Guggenheim Museum, *Richard Long*, 12 September – 30 November (see Publications).
London, Anthony d'Offay Gallery, *Richard Long: New Work*, 8 October – 12 November.
Pori, Finland, Porin Taidemuseo, *Richard Long*, 4 December 1986 – 25 January 1987.
Turin, Antonio Tucci Russo, *Richard Long*, 12 December 1986 – 14 March 1987.

1987
Geneva, Musée Rath, *Richard Long*, 7 May – 21 June (see Publications).

Liverpool, Renshaw Hall, *Allotment One: Richard Long –
Stone Field*, June, July, August.
Chicago, Donald Young Gallery, *Richard Long*,
23 October – 28 November (see Publications).
Nailsworth, Gloucestershire, Cairn Gallery, *Cairn:
Richard Long*, 7 November – 5 December.
Grenoble, Centre National d'Art Contemporain de
Grenoble Magasin, *Richard Long*, 13 December 1987 –
14 February 1988.
Athens, Jean Bernier, *Richard Long*, 15 December 1987 –
9 January 1988.

1988

Düsseldorf, Galerie Konrad Fischer, *Richard Long*, opened
20 February (duration approximately one month).
Aachen, Neue Galerie - Sammlung Ludwig, *3. Kunstpreis
Aachen: Richard Long*, 14 October – 20 November
(see Publications).
London, Anthony d'Offay Gallery, *Richard Long*,
22 October – 26 November.

1989

St. Gallen, Switzerland, Kunstverein St. Gallen,
Richard Long, 15 January – 26 February (see Publications).
Athens, Jean Bernier, *Richard Long*, 23 February –
27 March.
New York, Sperone Westwater, *Richard Long*,
18 March – 15 April.
Bristol, Coopers Gallery, Bristol Old Vic Theatre,
Footprints: Richard Long, 14 April – 27 May. Leaflet with
text by Rupert Martin.
Turin, Galleria Tucci Russo, *Richard Long*,
21 April – 20 July.
Chagny, France, Galerie Pietro Sparta, *Richard Long*,
10 June – 1 October.
La Jolla, California, La Jolla Museum of Contemporary
Art, *Richard Long*, 19/20 August – 15 October
(see Publications).
Halifax, Yorkshire, The Henry Moore Sculpture Trust
Studio, Dean Clough, *Richard Long: New Works*,
25 October – 10 December. Four postcards.

1990

Bristol, Arnolfini, *Richard Long*, 20 January – 25 February.
London, Anthony d'Offay Gallery, *Richard Long*,
26 January – 24 February (see Publications).

Los Angeles, Angles Gallery, *Richard Long: New work*,
23 March – 31 April.
Glarus, Switzerland, Galerie Tschudi, *Richard Long*,
7 July – 13 October.
Düsseldorf, Galerie Konrad Fischer, *Richard Long: Turf
Line*, opened 14 July (duration approximately one month).
London, Tate Gallery, *Richard Long*, 3 October 1990 –
6 January 1991. Brochure with text by Nicholas Serota.
Stockholm, Magasin 3 Stockholm Konsthall, *Richard Long*,
5 October 1990 – 30 January 1991. Catalogue, in Swedish and
English, with text by Roger Bevan.
Rochechouart, France, Château de Rochechouart, Musée
départemental d'art contemporain, *Richard Long*,
11 October 1990 – 6 January 1991 (see Publications).

1991

Liverpool, Tate Gallery Liverpool, *Richard Long*,
23 January – 3 March. Brochure with text by Nicholas
Serota (as London 1990).
Frankfurt, Städtische Galerie im Städelschen Kunstinstitut,
Richard Long, 21 February – 12 May (see Publications).
Turin, Galleria Tucci Russo, *Richard Long*,
27 February – 27 April.
London, Hayward Gallery, The South Bank Centre,
Richard Long: Walking in Circles, 14 June – 11 August
(see Publications).

SELECTED GROUP EXHIBITIONS

Unless otherwise noted, work was made for the first time
and for the exhibition cited, or it was made only for the
duration of the exhibition.

1967

Frankfurt, Dorothea Loehr, *19:45 – 21:55* (participating: Jan
Dibbets, Barry Flanagan, Bernhard Höke, John Johnson,
Richard Long, Konrad Lueg, Ch. Posenenske, Peter
Roehr), 9 September. Arranged by Paul Maenz. Catalogue.

1968

London, Royal Institute Galleries, *Young Contemporaries*,
30 January – 27 February. Brochure.
Amalfi, Festival of Free Expression, *A3: Arte e Azione
Povera*, October.

1969

Ithaca, New York, Cornell University, Andrew Dickson
White Museum of Art, *Earth Art*, 11 February – 16 March.
Catalogue with texts by Willoughby Sharp and William C.
Lipke and excerpts from a symposium moderated by
Thomas W. Leavitt and held with the artists on 6 February.
Amsterdam, Stedelijk Museum, *Op Losse Schroeven:
situaties en cryptostructuren*, 15 March – 27 April.
Catalogue, variously in Dutch, English and German, with
text in Dutch by Wim A. L. Beeren.
Berne, Kunsthalle, *Live in Your Head – When Attitudes
Become Form: Works – Concepts – Processes – Situations –
Information*, 22 March – 27 April; travelled to Krefeld,
Museum Haus Lange, 10 May – 25 June and, revised, to
London, Institute of Contemporary Arts, 28 September –
27 October. Catalogue, in English, German and French,
with texts by Harald Szeeman, Scott Burton, Grégoire
Muller, and Tommaso Trini; London catalogue by
Charles Harrison.
Düsseldorf, Fernsehgalerie Gerry Schum, "Land Art",
telecast in April by Sender Freies Berlin.

1970

Chicago, Museum of Contemporary Art, *Evidence on the
Flight of Six Fugitives*, 28 March – 10 May.
New York, The Museum of Modern Art, *Information*,
2 July – 20 September. Catalogue edited by
Kynaston L. McShine.

1971

New York, The Solomon R. Guggenheim Museum,
Guggenheim International Exhibition 1971,
12 February – 25 April. Catalogue with texts by
Diane Waldman and Edward F. Fry.
New York, The New York Cultural Center, *The British
Avant Garde*, 19 May – 29 August. Catalogue with texts by
Charles Harrison and Donald Karshan (in collaboration
with *Studio International*).
Arnhem, Park Sonsbeek, *Sonsbeek 71: Sonsbeek buiten de
perken*, 19 June – 15 August. Catalogue, in Dutch and
English, with text by W.A.L. Beeren. Richard Long
sculpture made at Pieterburen/Groningerwad.

1972

Kassel, Neue Galerie and Museum Fridericianum,
documenta 5: Befragung der Realität Bildwelten heute,

30 June – 8 October. Catalogue, in German. General Secretary: Harald Szeeman.
London, Hayward Gallery, *The New Art*, 17 August – 24 September. Catalogue with text by Anne Seymour.

1974
Brussels, Palais des Beaux-Arts, *Carl Andre, Marcel Broodthaers, Daniel Buren, Victor Burgin, Gilbert & George, On Kawara, Richard Long, Gerhard Richter*, 9 January – 3 February. Catalogue, in French and Flemish.

1975
Bristol, Arnolfini, *Artists Over Land*, 26 August – 20 September (Richard Long, Phillippa Ecobichon, Hamish Fulton, Marie Yates).

1976
Milan, Palazzo Reale, *Arte Inglese Oggi 1960 – 76*, 26 February – 16 May. Catalogue, in English and Italian; chapter including Long by Richard Cork.
Washington D.C., Corcoran Gallery of Art, *Andre/LeVa/Long*, 11 December 1976 – 30 January 1977. Catalogue with preface by Jane Livingston.

1977
Los Angeles, Los Angeles Institute of Contemporary Art, *Michael Asher, David Askevold, Richard Long*, 15 January – 10 February. Catalogue.
Münster, Westfälisches Landesmuseum für Kunst und Kulturgeschichte, *"Skulptur": Ausstellung in Münster 1977*, 3 July – 13 November. Catalogue, in German, in two volumes; Long included in volume 2, "Projektbereich".

1978
Penzance, Newlyn Art Gallery, *Peter Joseph, Richard Long, David Tremlett in Newlyn*, 17 January – 17 February. Three catalogues in one portfolio (see Publications).

1979
Paris, ARC Paris - Musée d'Art Moderne de la Ville de Paris, *Un Certain Art Anglais... Sélection d'artistes britanniques 1970-1979*, 19 January – 12 March. Catalogue, in French, with texts by Michael Compton, Richard Cork, and Sandy Nairne.
Berne, Kunsthalle, *Skulptur: Matisse, Giacometti, Judd, Flavin, Andre, Long*, 17 August – 23 September. Catalogue. (Work borrowed.)

1980
Humlebaek, Denmark, Louisiana Museum, *Andre, Dibbets, Long, Ryman*, 19 January – 24 February. Text on exhibition, in Danish, published in *Louisiana Revy*, volume 20, number 2, March 1980.
London, Hayward Gallery, *Pier + Ocean: Construction in the art of the seventies*, 8 May – 22 June; travelled to Otterlo, Rijksmuseum Kröller-Müller, 13 July – 8 September. Catalogue with text by Gerhard von Graevenitz.
St. Ives, Cornwall, St. Ives Summer Festival, *Roger Ackling, Hamish Fulton, Richard Long, Michael O'Donnell: Four Temporary Works Situated in West Penwith Cornwall England*, September. Catalogue with text by David Brown.

1981
Toyama, The Museum of Modern Art, *For a New Art: Toyama Now '81*, 5 July – 23 September. Catalogue, in English and Japanese; U.K. section by Michael Compton and including statement by the artist.
London, Whitechapel Art Gallery, *British Sculpture in the 20th Century. Part 2: Symbol and Imagination 1951-1980*, 27 November 1981 – 24 January 1982. Catalogue edited by Sandy Nairne and Nicholas Serota; chapter including Long by Stuart Morgan.

1982
Kassel, *documenta 7*, 19 June – 28 September. Catalogue, in 2 volumes, in German and English. Artistic Director: Rudi Fuchs.
Berlin, Nationalgalerie Staatliche Museen Preussischer Kulturbesitz, *Kunst wird Material*, 7 October – 5 December. Catalogue, in German, with texts by Michael Pauseback and Britta Schmitz.

1983
Helsinki, Art Museum of the Ateneum, *ARS 83 Helsinki*, opened 13 October. Catalogue, in Finnish.

1984
New Haven, Yale Center for British Art, *The Critical Eye/1: Victor Burgin, Gilbert & George, Mary Kelly, Richard Long, Bruce McLean, David Tremlett*, 16 May – 15 July. Catalogue with text by John T. Paoletti.
Dublin, The Guinness Hop Store, *ROSC '84: the poetry of vision*, 24 August – 17 November. Catalogue, including April 1984 statement by the artist and excerpt on Long from Michael Craig-Martin text in *Touchstones* (see Publications).
New York, The Museum of Modern Art, *"Primitivism" in 20th Century Art: Affinity of the Tribal and the Modern*, 24 September 1984 – 15 January 1985; travelled to Detroit Institute of Arts and to Dallas Museum of Art. Catalogue, in 2 volumes, edited by William Rubin; Long included in chapter by Kirk Varnedoe, volume 2.

1985
Turin, Castello di Rivoli, *Ouverture: Arte contemporanea* [n.d.]. Catalogue, in Italian and English, with text by Rudi Fuchs.

1986
London, Hayward Gallery, *Falls the Shadow: Recent British and European Art – 1986 Hayward Annual*, 9 April – 15 June. Catalogue with texts by Jon Thompson and Barry Barker.

1987
Edinburgh, Scottish Arts Council Touring Exhibition, *The Unpainted Landscape*; travelled to Ayr, Maclaurin Art Gallery, 10 January – 7 February; Stromness, Pier Arts Centre, 7 – 28 March; Edinburgh, Scottish National Gallery of Modern Art, 11 April – 17 May; Aberdeen, Artspace Galleries, 30 May – 24 June; Glasgow, University of Strathclyde, Collins Gallery, 7 July – 8 August; University of St. Andrews, Crawford Centre for the Arts, 21 August – 20 September. Accompanying book published by Coracle Press, Scottish Arts Council, and Graeme Murray Gallery; texts including Long by Simon Cutts and David Reason.
London, Royal Academy of Art, *British Art in the 20th Century: The Modern Movement*, 15 January – 5 April; travelled to Staatsgalerie Stuttgart. Catalogue edited by Susan Compton; chapter including Long by Richard Cork.
Stockholm, Liljevalchs Konsthall, *Art: Brittiskt 1980 – Tal*, 10 April – 24 May. Catalogue, in Swedish; text on Long by David Reason. (Organized by The British Council.)
Manchester, Cornerhouse, *Wall Works: Richard Long, Michael Craig-Martin, Annette Messager, Marion Möller, Matt Mullican, Sol LeWitt - Six artists working directly on the wall*, 14 November – 31 December. Brochure/poster with text by Maureen Paley.

1988

Liverpool, Tate Gallery Liverpool, *Starlit Waters: British Sculpture. An International Art 1968 – 1988*, 28 May 1988 – 4 September 1989. Catalogue; chapter including Long by Martin Kunz.

Reykjavik, *Donald Judd, Richard Long, Kristján Gudmundsson*, Nylistasafnid, The Living Art Museum, 4 – 19 June. Catalogue, in Icelandic, with preface by Pitur Arason.

Cambridge, England, Jesus College, *Sculpture in the Close*, 20 June – 31 July. Catalogue with text by Colin Renfrew.

Saint Louis, The Saint Louis Art Museum, *New Sculpture/Six Artists (Currents 37)*, 23 September – 30 October. Catalogue with text on Richard Long by Maureen Megerian and Daniel A. Reich.

1989

Paris, Musée national d'art moderne - Centre Georges Pompidou and Grande Halle - La Villette, *Magiciens de la Terre*, 18 May – 14 August. Catalogue, in French.

New York, The Solomon R. Guggenheim Museum, *Selections from the Permanent Collection*, 18 July – 3 September.

Turin, Aboreto dell'Orto Botanico, *Hortus Artis: Mostre d'Arte in Orti Botanici*, opened 14 September. Organized by Castello di Rivoli.

Istanbul, Süleymaniye Imaret (Süleymaniye Cultural Centre), *2. Istanbul Bienali*, 25 September - 31 October. Catalogue, in Turkish and English; chapter including Long by Beral Madra.

1990

Oslo, Wang Kunsthandel, *3 + 1: Paul Brand, Terje Roalkvam, Dag Skedsmo, Richard Long*, 13 January – 11 February. Catalogue, in Norwegian, with text by Sune Nordgren.

Lincoln, Lincoln Cathedral, *The Journey*, 17 June – 12 August.

Bordeaux, capcMusée d'Art Contemporain de Bordeaux, *Collection: Christian Boltanski, Daniel Buren, Gilbert & George, Jannis Kounellis, Sol LeWitt, Richard Long, Mario Merz*, 29 June – 30 December. Catalogue, in French; texts on Long by Michel Bourel, Paco Calvo Serraller, and Marcel Cohen.

Paris, Galerie Ghislaine Hussenot, *Time, Space, Place: Richard Long, On Kawara, Lawrence Weiner*, 8 September – 18 October.

Tourcoing, France, Musée des Beaux-Arts de Tourcoing, *Le Diaphane: Une Réflexion, Une Collection, Une Exposition, Un Lieu*, 24 November 1990 – 2 February 1991.

1991

Madrid, Galeria Weber, Alexander y Cobo, *Hamish Fulton, Richard Long*, 6 February – 30 March. Catalogue.

London, Anthony d'Offay Gallery, *Bronze, Steel, Stone, Wood: Carl Andre, Ellsworth Kelly, Richard Long – Three Installations of Sculpture*, 5 March – 13 April.

PUBLICATIONS ON AND BY THE ARTIST

RICHARD LONG SKULPTUREN
Städtisches Museum Mönchengladbach, Mönchengladbach, 1970. Text by Johannes Cladders and statement by the artist (on occasion of exhibition)

From along a Riverbank: Richard Long
Art & Project, Amsterdam, August 1971

Two sheepdogs cross in and out of the passing shadows The clouds drift over the hill with a storm: Richard Long
Lisson Publications, London, Summer 1971

JOHN BARLEYCORN
Stedelijk Museum, Amsterdam, 1973
(on occasion of exhibition)

From Around a Lake: Richard Long
Art & Project, Amsterdam, August 1973

RICHARD LONG: SOUTH AMERICA 1972
Konrad Fischer, Düsseldorf [1973]; reissued, in Swedish, by Kalejdoskop, Lund, 1978

INCA ROCK CAMPFIRE ASH: RICHARD LONG
Scottish National Gallery of Modern Art, Edinburgh, 1974 (on occasion of exhibition)

THE NORTH WOODS: RICHARD LONG
Whitechapel Art Gallery, London, 1977 (on occasion of exhibition)

A HUNDRED STONES: RICHARD LONG CORNWALL ENGLAND 1977
Kunsthalle, Berne, 1977 (on occasion of exhibition)

A STRAIGHT HUNDRED MILE WALK IN AUSTRALIA: RICHARD LONG 1977
John Kaldor Project 6 [Australia], 1977 (on occasion of exhibition)

RIVERS AND STONES: RICHARD LONG
Newlyn Orion Galleries, Cornwall, 1978 (on occasion of group exhibition)

RIVER AVON BOOK: RICHARD LONG
Anthony d'Offay Gallery, London, 1979 (exhibition to mark publication)

RICHARD LONG
Van Abbemuseum, Eindhoven, 1979 (on occasion of exhibition)

Richard Long in *Aggie Weston's*
Coracle Press, London, No. 16, Winter 1979

A WALK PAST STANDING STONES: RICHARD LONG
Anthony d'Offay Gallery, London, 1979; Coracle Press for Anthony d'Offay, 1980

RICHARD LONG: Five, six, pick up sticks Seven, eight, lay them straight
Anthony d'Offay Gallery, London, 1980. Statement by the artist (on occasion of exhibition)

TWELVE WORKS 1979 – 1981: RICHARD LONG
Anthony d'Offay Gallery, London, 1981 (on occasion of exhibition)

RICHARD LONG BORDEAUX 1981
Centre d'Arts Plastiques Contemporains de Bordeaux, 1982 (following 1981 exhibition)

SELECTED WORKS OEUVRES CHOISIES 1979 – 1982: RICHARD LONG
National Gallery of Canada, Ottawa, 1982 (on occasion of exhibition)

MEXICO 1979: RICHARD LONG
Van Abbemuseum, Eindhoven, 1982

TOUCHSTONES: RICHARD LONG
Arnolfini, Bristol, 1983. Statement by the artist, 'Words After the Fact 1982', and text by Michael Craig-Martin (on occasion of exhibition)

FANGO PIETRE LEGNI: RICHARD LONG
Antonio Tucci Russo, Turin, 1983
(on occasion of exhibition)

COUNTLESS STONES: RICHARD LONG
Van Abbemuseum, Eindhoven, and Openbaar
Kunstbezit, 1983

PLANES OF VISION RICHARD LONG ENGLAND 1983
Ottenhausen Verlag, Aachen, 1983

RICHARD LONG: POSTCARDS 1968 – 1982
capcMusée d'Art Contemporain de Bordeaux, 1983; corrected
and reprinted 1984

RICHARD LONG
Century Cultural Foundation, Tokyo, 1984. Titles in
Japanese and English (following 1983 exhibition)

RIVER AVON MUD WORKS: RICHARD LONG
Orchard Gallery, Londonderry, 1984
(on occasion of exhibition)

SIXTEEN WORKS: RICHARD LONG
Anthony d'Offay Gallery, London, 1984
(on occasion of exhibition)

MUD HAND PRINTS: RICHARD LONG
Coracle Press, London, May 1984

IL LUOGO BUONO: RICHARD LONG
Padiglione d'Arte Contemporanea di Milano, 1985. Texts by
Marco Meneguzzo (in English and Italian) and Anne
Seymour (in Italian) (on occasion of exhibition)

RICHARD LONG
Fonds Régional d'Art Contemporain Aquitaine, 1985 (on
occasion of its acquisition of LIGNE D'ARDOISE BORDEAUX 1985,
installed at capcMusée d'Art Contemporain de Bordeaux)

MUDDY WATER MARKS: RICHARD LONG
MW Press, Noordwijk, Holland, 1985

RICHARD LONG IN CONVERSATION
MW Press, Noordwijk, Holland, 1985 (with Martina
Giezen. Part 1: Bristol, 19 November 1985; Part 2: London,
7 April 1986 and Amsterdam, 13 April 1986)

PIEDRAS: RICHARD LONG
Ministerio de Cultura, Madrid, and The British Council,
1986. Text by Anne Seymour, in Spanish (translation of text
in *Il Luogo Buono*, 1985) (on occasion of exhibition at
Palacio de Cristal)

RICHARD LONG
Thames and Hudson, Ltd., London, and The Solomon R.
Guggenheim Foundation, New York, 1986. Text by R.H.
Fuchs (on occasion of exhibition)

LINES OF TIME/TIJDLIJNEN
Stichting Edy de Wilde-Lezing, Amsterdam, 1986 (lecture –
slide show with music – by Richard Long on 19 November
at the Vondelkerk, Amsterdam; in Dutch and English)

STONE WATER MILES: RICHARD LONG
Musée Rath, Geneva, 1987. Text by Hendel Teicher, in
French (on occasion of exhibition)

OUT OF THE WIND: RICHARD LONG
Donald Young Gallery, Chicago, 1987
(on occasion of exhibition)

DUST DOBROS DESERT FLOWERS: RICHARD LONG
The Lapis Press, Los Angeles, 1987

RICHARD LONG: OLD WORLD NEW WORLD
Anthony d'Offay Gallery, London, and Verlag der
Buchhandlung Walther König, Cologne, 1988. Text by
Anne Seymour (revised version of text in *Il Luogo Buono*,
1985). Published to commemorate the award of the
Kunstpreis Aachen Neue Galerie – Sammlung Ludwig,
14 October 1988 (also see One-man exhibitions)

RICHARD LONG: ANGEL FLYING TOO CLOSE TO THE GROUND
Kunstverein St. Gallen, Switzerland, 1989
(on occasion of exhibition)

SURF ROAR: RICHARD LONG
La Jolla Museum of Contemporary Art, La Jolla,
California, 1989. Text by Hugh M. Davies
(on occasion of exhibition)

KICKING STONES: RICHARD LONG
Anthony d'Offay Gallery, London, 1990
(on occasion of exhibition)

RICHARD LONG: SUR LA ROUTE
Musée départemental de Rochechouart, Rochechouart,
France, 1990. Text by Guy Tosatto, in French
(on occasion of exhibition)

NILE: PAPERS OF RIVER MUD
The Lapis Press, Los Angeles, 1990

RICHARD LONG: LABYRINTH
Städtische Galerie im Städelschen Kunstinstitut , Frankfurt,
1991 (on occasion of exhibition)

RICHARD LONG: WALKING IN CIRCLES
Hayward Gallery, The South Bank Centre, London, 1991.
Texts by Anne Seymour and Hamish Fulton and transcript
of 1988 radio interview with Richard Cork
(on occasion of exhibition)

FILMS ON AND BY THE ARTIST

WALKING A STRAIGHT LINE TEN MILES LONG
OUT AND BACK DARTMOOR ENGLAND 1969.
6 minutes 33 seconds, colour, sound. Made for "Land Art",
Fernsehgalerie Gerry Schum, and telecast in April 1969 by
Sender Freies Berlin.

RICHARD LONG.
"Omnibus", BBC Television, Autumn 1982.

STONES AND FLIES Richard Long in the Sahara.
Directed and produced by Philip Haas. A Methodact
Production for the Arts Council of Great Britain in
association with Channel 4 Television, HPS Films Berlin
and Centre Pompidou, La SEPT, CNAP, and WDR, 1988.

INDEX OF WORKS AND PHOTOGRAPHIC CREDITS

The following is an alphabetical index of works reproduced in this book. Titles are given in capital letters. Untitled works are listed in alphabetical sequence but are individually distinguished by reference to the gallery in which they were installed, as are works with the same title done in the same year. The title is followed by the date of the work and details of its medium. Dimensions for sculptures are given. Unless otherwise stated, photographs are by Richard Long.

Note: Richard Long went to the Sahara twice in 1988, the first time to make a walk alone in the Hoggar mountains, the second time with a small film crew to make "STONES AND FLIES" in the same area as his walk.

ACKNOWLEDGEMENTS

Richard Long has on three occasions made work specially for exhibitions in the Hayward Gallery: THREE CIRCLES OF STONES for Anne Seymour's celebrated *The New Art* in 1972; STONE LINE for *Pier + Ocean* in 1980; and FALLS OF MUDDY WATER for *Falls the Shadow: Recent British and European Art* in 1986. They have been amongst the most memorable works installed in the galleries. We are therefore delighted to present this one-man exhibition, occupying the entire gallery, the fullest showing of Long's work in this country since his retrospective at the Whitechapel Art Gallery in 1977.

Richard Long has been tirelessly involved with every aspect of the selection and installation of the exhibition and this accompanying publication. It has been a pleasure to work with him.

This book has been conceived to complement the exhibition rather than as an exhibition catalogue in the conventional sense. It is the most substantial publication on Long's work to date, and in particular concentrates on work produced since his exhibition at The Solomon R. Guggenheim Museum in New York in 1986. We are indebted to Anne Seymour and to Hamish Fulton for the texts they have contributed, which reflect their long and close association with the artist. Our thanks go too to Richard Cork and Judith Bumpus for permission to print the interview Richard Long and Richard Cork made for Radio 3. Herman Lelie has worked energetically and devotedly with Richard Long on the design of the book. The staff of the Tate Gallery Library kindly made the library available to us for the compilation of documentary material.

The exhibition could not have been realized without the generous sponsorship of Beck's Bier. Their continuing, enlightened support of the Hayward Gallery in recent years is a fine example of how business can best contribute to contemporary art.

We are also most grateful for the support of The Henry Moore Foundation. We would like to thank as well the Anthony d'Offay Gallery and Richard Long for their assistance with this publication.

The Anthony d'Offay Gallery has helped with numerous aspects of the project. We would particularly like to thank Anthony d'Offay, Lorcan O'Neill, Tanya Bonakdar, Sadie Coles and Robert Violette.

Not least, we are grateful to the lenders to the exhibition, those listed on the opposite page and those who wish to remain anonymous, who responded to our loan requests with a generosity and enthusiasm that indicates the esteem and affection in which Richard Long and his work are held.

Joanna Drew
Director, Hayward and Regional Exhibitions

Susan Ferleger Brades
Senior Exhibition Organizer

I would especially like to thank Hamish Fulton for being a good friend and fellow-traveller, and for taking the photograph of me on the road in Peru.
R.L.

LENDERS TO THE EXHIBITION

Kazuo Akao
Brooke and Carolyn Alexander, New York
Caroline and Dick Anderson
Collection Becht, Naarden, Holland
Cristina and Thomas Bechtler, Switzerland
Edwin C. Cohen, New York
Paolo Consolandi
Crex Collection, Hallen für neue Kunst, Schaffhausen, Switzerland
Collection Deslypere – Pannier, Ghent – Dallas
Anne and Anthony d'Offay
Fay, Richwhite, Auckland, New Zealand
Marie-Louise Laband
Melia Marden
Collection Panza di Biumo
Hester van Royen, London
Collection Sanders, Amsterdam
Gilbert and Lila Silverman, Detroit, Michigan
Daniel and Danielle Varenne
Jack and Nell Wendler
Mike and Penny Winton
The Worthington Collection (Lent by Greville Worthington)

Anthony d'Offay Gallery, London
Art & Project, NL – Slootdorp
Konrad Fischer, Düsseldorf
Galerie Löhrl, Mönchengladbach
Galeria Marga Paz, Madrid
Karsten Schubert Ltd., London
Galerie Pietro Sparta, Chagny
Galerie Tschudi, Glarus

The British Council
Museum van Hedendaagse Kunst, Ghent
The Museum of Contemporary Art, Helsinki, Finland
The Trustees of the Tate Gallery, London
Southampton City Art Gallery

WITHDRAWN

Originally published on the occasion of the exhibition
RICHARD LONG: WALKING IN CIRCLES,
at the Hayward Gallery, The South Bank Centre, London, 1991

EXHIBITION SPONSORED BY BECK'S BIER

Exhibition supported by The Henry Moore Foundation

Exhibition and publication organized by
Susan Ferleger Brades
Assisted by Annabel Parmenter

Designed by Richard Long and Herman Lelie

Typeset by Goodfellow & Egan Phototypesetting Ltd., Cambridge
Produced in Germany by Uwe Kraus GmbH, Murr/Stuttgart

Any copy of this book issued by the publisher as a paperback is sold
subject to the condition that it shall not by way of trade or otherwise be
lent, resold, hired out or otherwise circulated without the publisher's
prior consent in any form of binding or cover than that in which it is
published and without a similar condition including these words being
imposed on a subsequent purchaser

Text © 1991 The South Bank Centre and the authors
'OLD MUDDY' © 1991 Hamish Fulton
Illustrations © 1991 Richard Long

Originally published in paperback in 1991
by Thames and Hudson Ltd, London
Reprinted 1994

All rights reserved. No part of this publication may be reproduced
or transmitted in any form or by any means, electronic or
mechanical, including photocopy, recording or any other
information storage and retrieval system, without prior
permission in writing from the publisher

British Library Cataloguing-in Publication Data
A catalogue record for this book is available from the British Library

ISBN 0-500-27650-1

Printed and bound in Germany

Front cover: DUSTY BOOTS CIRCLE THE SAHARA 1988
Endpapers: RIVER AVON MUD DRAWINGS 1990
Half title: MUD HAND CIRCLES
MEMORIAL SLOAN-KETTERING CANCER CENTER NEW YORK 1989
Frontispiece: Richard Long walking in The Sahara 1988
Back cover: HOGGAR CIRCLE THE SAHARA 1988

WITHDRAWN

WITHDRAWN

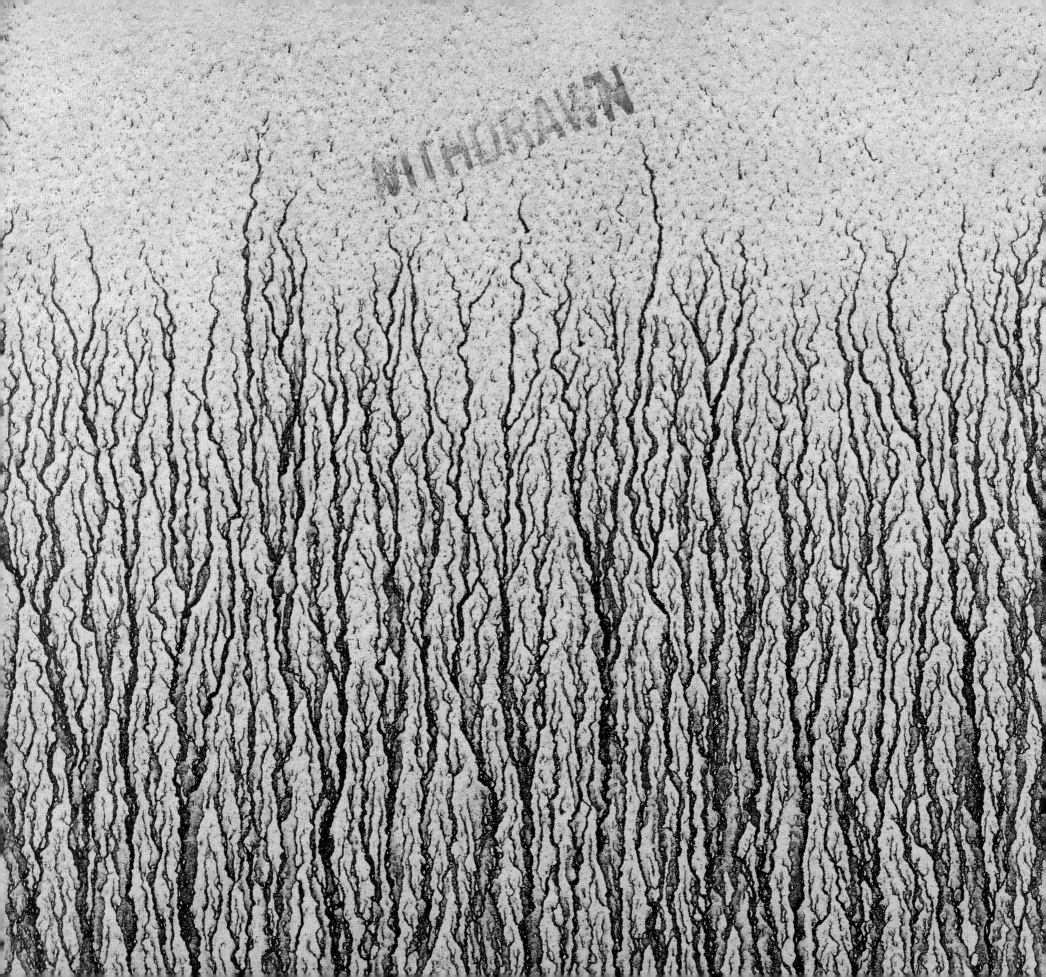

WITHDRAWN

Another copy
A&E m.e.

WITHDRAWN